FREE TRADE,
PROTECTION AND CUSTOMS UNION

PUBLICATION OF THE
ECONOMISCH SOCIOLOGISCH INSTITUUT - TILBURG

FREE TRADE, PROTECTION
AND
CUSTOMS UNION

by

L. H. JANSSEN, S. J.

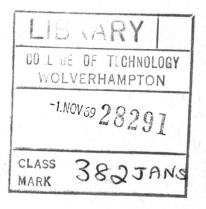
1961

H. E. STENFERT KROESE N.V. — LEIDEN

Printed in the Netherlands

ACKNOWLEDGEMENTS

This book is the result of a research project, started at the Economisch Sociologisch Instituut at Tilburg, The Netherlands. Prof. Schouten put me on the trail of Verdoorn's stimulating paper, read to the Netherlands Economic Society in 1952. This paper, written in Dutch, was never translated, but two alternative versions were published in English*. Although the present book took its origin from a criticism of Verdoorn's work, it will be clear to the reader how much the author is indebted to Verdoorn's original approach.

Most of all, however, I owe a debt of gratitude to Prof. Schouten. Even before I started this book he deeply influenced my economic thinking, and many of the methods used are in fact directly or indirectly borrowed from his teaching. I am sure that without his stimulating and encouraging guidance this book would never have been finished.

I should also like to thank all who have helped in any way to bring this book to completion. Particular acknowledgements are due to the Board of Directors of the Economisch Sociologisch Instituut at Tilburg, for placing so many facilities at my disposal. Mr. A. Smulders and Mr. J. Hilhorst not only helped me in practical ways but gave me encouragement by their neverfailing interest and willingness to co-operate. In the many calculations involved I was assisted at an early stage by the Statistical Department of the State Mines. I am indebted to Mr. G. E. Luton for his English translation, and to Miss N. Boers for the care and devotion with which she prepared the manuscript and read the proofs.

Finally, I should like to thank Professors Dalmulder, De Roos, Tinbergen and Verdoorn for reading the manuscript and for their helpful criticism.

* For references see pp. 64, 67 and 77.

CONTENTS

CHAPTER I

INTERNATIONAL TRADE
WITH ONE SCARCE PRODUCTION FACTOR

Since Adam Smith it has been a commonplace of economic theory that international trade can raise the general level of prosperity. In re-examining this well known theory here, we do so with the object of illustrating the method that will be used in the later chapters as an approach to economic integration.

International trade, like all trade, is governed by supply and demand. The demand depends on income and on preferences which are assumed to be known. The supply contains, as autonomous elements, technology and the amount of available production factors. By technology we mean the technically feasible methods of production or briefly techniques. The techniques will be denoted by the quantity of production factors required per unit product.

To begin as simply as possible, we assume in this chapter that there is only one scarce production factor — labour. Further, we shall confine ourselves to a two-country, two-product model. Two countries, 1 and 2, can each make two products, C and I. The labour force is assumed to be immobile, so that the available amount of labour is given for both countries. As regards technology in both countries, three assumptions can be made:

1. Technologies are identical in both countries;
2. Technologies are not identical, but the ratio of the amount of labour required per C product to that required per I product is identical in both countries;
3. This ratio is also not identical.

IDENTICAL COSTS STRUCTURE

For our purpose the first and second cases are not essentially different: in both cases international trade will yield no advantage. A country derives advantage from trade only when goods are obtained by exchange at less cost than if it were to produce those goods itself. In a two-product model the costs of the C product may be defined as the quantity of the I product that would have to be forgone in order to produce one unit of the C product. This may also be called the marginal substitution ratio or the opportunity cost.

A country will be prepared to exchange its own C product for the I product of another country only if the real terms of trade $\frac{C}{I}$ are smaller than, or at least equal to, its own marginal substitution ratio of C and I. Conversely, the other country will not be willing to part with its I product unless it obtains at least no less or more of the C product in exchange than it would have been able to make itself with the production factors it has invested in the I product.

If the opportunity cost or the marginal substitution ratio is the same in both countries, neither party has anything to gain, because the most favourable offer from the partner is no more advantageous than the alternative, which consists in producing both goods at home. The situation referred to is illustrated graphically in figure 1.

Graphic Representation

The C product is set out on the vertical axis and the I product on the horizontal axis. All values are positive and in the first quadrant they relate to country 2 and in the third quadrant to country 1. The line section OA indicates how much C product could be made in country 2 if all the available labour L^2 * were used for C production in country 2. Let α_c^2 be the amount of labour required in country 2 to produce one C unit, then the section $OA = \frac{L^2}{\alpha_c^2}$. Likewise $OB = \frac{L^2}{\alpha_i^2}$, where α_i^2 is the amount of labour required to produce one I unit (subscript i) in country 2 (superscript 2). The line AB, called the transformation line of labour, has a slope given by $\frac{L^2}{\alpha_c^2} : \frac{L^2}{\alpha_i^2} = \frac{\alpha_i^2}{\alpha_c^2}$. This line indicates what combinations of C and I can be achieved in country 2 with the

* Superscripts denote the country, and subscripts the product.

available amount of labour and existing techniques. Similarly, in the third quadrant the line CD is the transformation line of labour in country 1.

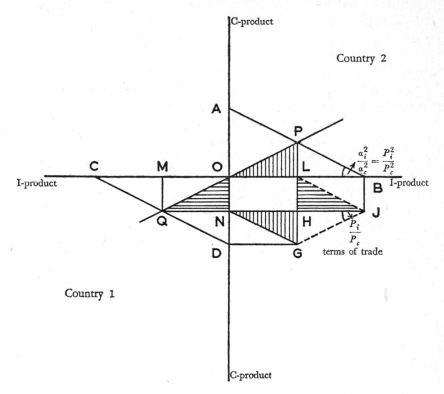

Figure 1. Autarky and free trade, indentical technologies

With regard to the demand we assume that in country 2 a fixed proportion of income γ^2 is spent on C products (one might conveniently call this the consumption share *) and the remainder, $1 - \gamma^2$, on I products. This 'expenditure function' is denoted by the line OP, whose slope can easily be shown ** to be equal to

* Although C and I are the initial letters of consumers' and investment goods, they need not always represent these categories of goods.
** See D. B. J. Schouten, *Exacte Economie*, Leiden 1957, page 8.

$\dfrac{\gamma^2}{1-\gamma^2} \cdot \dfrac{P_i^2}{P_c^2}$. It is further assumed that the fixed proportions of income spent on C and I (the expenditure shares) in country 1 are the same as in country 2.

The price ratio is determined in the case of autarky by the cost ratio, indicated by the slopes of the transformation lines. This is evident, since these slopes indicate how much C product must be forgone in order to make one more I product. The effective demand and the effective supply are governed finally by the points of intersection of the demand and supply curves. In the figure, in the case of autarky, country 2 will produce and consume a quantity PL of the C product and a quantity OL of the I product. Country 1 produces and consumes QM of the C product and OM of the I product.

Model 1.1 Autarky

The foregoing can be represented as follows in an extremely simple model consisting of a supply equation (being the expression of the transformation line AB), a demand equation (being the expression of the demand function OP), two price equations and two equilibrium equations. With the aid of these six equations we can solve the six variables, viz. two production volumes, two expenditure volumes and two prices.

$$X_c^1 = \frac{L^1}{\alpha_c^1} - \frac{\alpha_i^1}{\alpha_c^1} X_i^1 \quad \dots \dots \dots \dots \quad (1)$$

$$S_c^1 = \frac{\gamma^1}{1-\gamma^1} \cdot \frac{P_i^1}{P_c^1} S_i^1 \quad \dots \dots \dots \quad (2)$$

$$P_c^1 = \alpha_c^1 P_L^1 \quad \dots \dots \dots \dots \dots \quad (3)$$

$$P_i^1 = \alpha_i^1 P_L^1 \quad \dots \dots \dots \dots \dots \quad (4)$$

$$S_c^1 = X_c^1 \quad \dots \dots \dots \dots \dots \quad (5)$$

$$S_i^1 = X_i^1 \quad \dots \dots \dots \dots \dots \quad (6)$$

X_c^1 = volume of C production
S_c^1 = volume of expenditure on the C product
X_i^1 = volume of I production
S_i^1 = volume of expenditure on the I product
L^1 = available quantity of labour
P_L^1 = wage rate
P_i^1 = price of I product
P_c^1 = price of C product

All quantities relate to country 1 (superscript 1). A similar model applies to country 2.

Numerical Example

Given: $L^1 = 20$; $\alpha_c^1 = 2$; $\alpha_i^1 = 1$; $\gamma^1 = 0.5$; $P_L^1 = 1$
$\qquad L^2 = 40$; $\alpha_c^2 = 4$; $\alpha_i^2 = 2$; $\gamma^2 = 0.5$; $P_L^2 = 0.5$

Substitution of these data in the foregoing equations yields the solutions:

$$X_c^1 = 5;\ X_i^1 = 10;\ S_c^1 = 5;\ S_i^1 = 10;\ P_c^1 = 2;\ P_i^1 = 1$$
$$X_c^2 = 5;\ X_i^2 = 10;\ S_c^2 = 5;\ S_i^2 = 10;\ P_c^2 = 2;\ P_i^2 = 1$$

These results may be reproduced as follows in a confrontation table of resources and expenditure.

AUTARKY, IDENTICAL TECHNOLOGIES

Country 1

Resources	Volume	Price	Value	Expend-iture	Volume	Price	Value
X_c^1	5	× 2	= 10	S_c^1	5	× 2	= 10
X_i^1	10	× 1	= 10	S_i^1	10	× 1	= 10
L^1	20	× 1	= 20				20

Country 2

Resources	Volume	Price	Value	Expend-iture	Volume	Price	Value
X_c^2	5	× 2	= 10	S_c^2	5	× 2	= 10
X_i^2	10	× 1	= 10	S_i^2	10	× 1	= 10
L^2	40	× 0.5	= 20				20

COMPLETE SPECIALIZATION AND FREE TRADE

Let us now assume that the two countries wish to abandon their autarkic position and enter into trade. Country 1 starts to specialize in C production. Why it does so is not clear; it might equally specialize in I production . . . with just as little success. Assume then that country 1 specializes completely in C production. It will produce the quantity OD (see fig. 1). Of this quantity, according to the consumption share ($\gamma^1 = 0.5$), it will itself consume one half ON = LH. The remainder, ND = HG, it will be prepared to exchange for a quantity of I products that must be at least twice as large as the quantity HG, because country 1 is able itself to produce two I products for every C product it forgoes.

On the other hand, country 2 must now specialize in I production. In that case it produces the quantity OB, of which it consumes one half, OL = NH. It is willing to exchange the remainder, LB = HJ, for C products provided they amount to at least half of the quantity HJ, because country 2 possesses the alternative of producing half an I product instead of one C product.

These considerations, then, establish the real terms of trade $\dfrac{C}{I}$, which are equal to the nominal terms of trade $\dfrac{P_i}{P_e}$. In the case discussed, where the ratio of the labour inputs per unit of C and I products is equal in both countries, there is no profit to be gained by either country, because the maximum offer of the other is no more advantageous than the alternative, which consists in producing the product oneself. In fig. 1 this is illustrated by the 'expenditure triangles', LHJ for country 1 and NHG for country 2. These are equal to the 'expenditure triangles' that applied under autarky, namely QNO for country 1 and OLP for country 2. International trade has thus yielded no real advantage.

To begin with the simplest case we have chosen our quantities in such a way as to have complete specialization in both countries. We shall return later to the case of incomplete specialization.

Numerical Example of Complete Specialization
Since this is a very special case, we shall not try to express it in terms of a model (see page 15).

Nevertheless, it may be useful as an illustration to work out the case of complete specialization in a numerical example, as done for the case of autarky.

First, we can calculate the production point of country 1 (point D in figure 1). Country 1 specializes in C production. The quantity it produces is equal to the available quantity of labour (L^1) divided by the quantity of labour needed per unit product (α_c^1).

In our case, then, the production figure is 10. In accordance with the existing preference $(\gamma^1 = 0.5)$ half the country's income is spent on its own C product.

Since the income arises exclusively from the production of C, half the income will buy half of the real C product: hence the real expenditure on C goods amounts to 5. The remainder of the production is exported in exchange for the I product of country 2. This country in its turn produces $40 : 2 = 20$ I products, it consumes half itself $(1 - \gamma^2 = \frac{1}{2})$ and exports the other 10 I products. The terms of trade are now 5 C products for 10 I products, hence $\frac{P_i}{P_c} = \frac{1}{2}$. This is exactly the price ratio that would have prevailed if both countries had remained autarkic. If this ratio were greater than $\frac{1}{2}$, the autarkic state would be more favourable for country 1; if it were smaller than $\frac{1}{2}$, country 2 would undoubtedly return to a state of autarky.

The nominal level of P_i and P_c in a given country is determined by the nominal wage level of that country. A nominal price difference compared with the other country then appears in a rate of exchange differing from unity. In our example the wage rates are so chosen as to give an exchange rate of 1. In other words $P_i^1 = P_i^2$ and $P_c^1 = P_c^2$. The results can now be represented in a confrontation table of resources and expenditure.

FREE TRADE, COMPLETE SPECIALIZATION

Country 1

Resources	Volume	Price	Value	Expend-iture	Volume	Price	Value
X_c^1	10	× 2	= 20	S_c^1	5	× 2	= 10
X_i^1	0	× 1	= 0	S_i^1	10	× 1	= 10
L^1	20	× 1	= 20				20
Imports M_i^1	10	× 1	= 10	Exports F_c^1	5	× 2	= 10

Country 2

Resources	Volume	Price	Value	Expend-iture	Volume	Price	Value
X_c^2	0	× 2	= 0	S_c^2	5	× 2	= 10
X_i^2	20	× 1	= 20	S_i^2	10	× 1	= 10
L^2	40	× 0.5	= 20				20
Imports M_c^2	5	× 2	= 10	Exports F_i^2	10	× 1	= 10

Comparison of this table with the preceding one, which applied in the case of autarky, shows that neither of the two countries benefits: the expenditure remains exactly the same. Nevertheless, there is a distinct difference in technology.

*The advantage of international trade does not, however, result from a
difference in technical skill alone, but from a difference in relative or comparative costs.*

Mobility

The difference in technology referred to above is indeed of importance, however, if mobility of labour exists. In that case,
labour will move to that country where the quantities of labour
needed per unit of product are lower, in other words where the
real wage is higher. If capital remains abundant the one country
will be depleted of labour and the wages thus levelled out. On the
other hand, if capital becomes scarce in the rich country, labour in
that country will become abundant, which again leads to wage
levelling. Where labour is not mobile, however, international trade
(still working on the above assumptions) will have no levelling
effect on wages.

COSTS STRUCTURE NOT IDENTICAL

Dissimilar technologies can lead, however, to dissimilar cost ratios
(case 3). For the moment, we shall leave out of account the difference in costs that arise from differences in the relative scarcity of
capital and labour. We are still considering labour, it will be remembered, as the only scarce factor.

Let the cost ratios be given by the following technical data:

$$\alpha_c^1 = 1 \qquad\qquad \alpha_c^2 = 2$$
$$\alpha_i^1 = 2 \qquad\qquad \alpha_i^2 = 1$$

We also have $L^1 = 60$, $L^2 = 80$, and equal expenditure shares in both
countries: $\gamma^1 = \gamma^2 = 0.5$. The wage rate is immaterial for our present
purposes, since the wage rate only determines the price *level*, not the
proportions of prices. P_L^1 is put at 1, P_L^2 at 0.75.

These data are set forth in the form of a graph in fig. 2. Under
autarky, the transformation curves are AB and CD, the expenditure
curves OP and OQ. The points of intersection P and Q denote the
production and expenditure points. Substitution of the data in
model 1.1 gives the following confrontation table of resources and
expenditure.

AUTARKY, DISSIMILAR TECHNOLOGIES

Country 1

Resources	Volume	Price	Value	Expend-iture	Volume	Price	Value
X_c^1	30	× 1	= 30	S_c^1	30	× 1	= 30
X_i^1	15	× 2	= 30	S_i^1	15	× 2	= 30
L^1	60	× 1	= 60				60

Country 2

Resources	Volume	Price	Value	Expen-diture	Volume	Price	Value
X_c^2	20	× 1.5	= 30	S_c^2	20	× 1.5	= 30
X_i^2	40	× 0.75	= 30	S_i^2	40	× 0.75	= 30
L^2	80	× 0.75	= 60				60

The joint production, and also the real expenditure of each country individually, can now be raised by specialization. In the case of autarky the total production consists of 50 C products and 55 I products. If country 1 specializes in C production and country 2 in I production, they can produce respectively 60 C products and 80 I products, indicated in the figure by OD and OB. Of the quantity OD, country 1, following the existing preference, will want to retain half, ON = LH, for its own use and will be prepared to exchange the other half ND = HG for the I product of country 2. Similarly, country 2 is prepared to exchange the quantity LB = HJ of its own product for the C product of country 1. The resultant real terms of trade $\dfrac{C}{I}$, which must be equal to the nominal terms of trade $\dfrac{P_i}{P_c}$, are denoted in the figure by the tangent of the angle HJG.

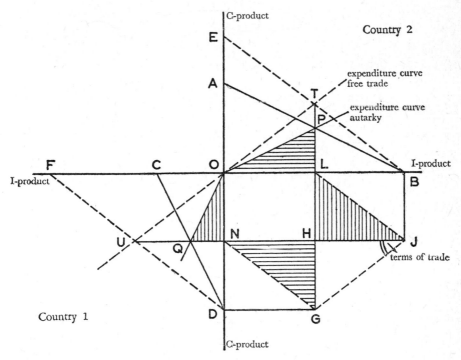

Figure 2. Autarky and free trade, dissimilar technologies

The expenditure can be read from the figure as the 'expenditure triangles' NHG and HLJ. These expenditure triangles are also drawn in the first and third quadrants as OLT and UNO. The expenditure point T is the point of intersection of the international exchange line EB with the expenditure line applicable in country 2 to free trade, and which has a steeper slope than the autarkic expenditure line because, in the case of free trade, the price ratio

$\dfrac{P_i}{P_c} = \tfrac{3}{4}$ is greater than the price ratio under autarky $\dfrac{P_i^2}{P_c^2} = \tfrac{1}{2}$. This

is evident since the expenditure line is equal to $\dfrac{\gamma}{1-\gamma}\dfrac{P_i}{P_c}$.

The expenditure triangle OLT is plainly larger than the original triangle OLP. In country 1, also, ONU is larger than ONQ.

Model 1.2   *Complete Specialization*

The model is particularly simple and consists of two production equations, two expenditure equations and two equilibrium equations, from which we can solve the six variables, viz. two production and four expenditure volumes. Two price equations can also be added here.

$$X_c^1 = \frac{L^1}{\alpha_c^1} \quad \dots \dots \dots \dots \dots \dots \quad (1)$$

$$X_i^2 = \frac{L^2}{\alpha_i^2} \quad \dots \dots \dots \dots \dots \dots \quad (2)$$

$$S_c^1 = \gamma^1 X_c^1 \dots \dots \dots \dots \dots \dots \quad (3)$$

$$S_i^2 = (1 - \gamma^2) X_i^2 \dots \dots \dots \dots \dots \quad (4)$$

$$X_c^1 = S_c^1 + S_c^2 \dots \dots \dots \dots \dots \dots \quad (5)$$

$$X_i^2 = S_i^1 + S_i^2 \dots \dots \dots \dots \dots \dots \quad (6)$$

$$\frac{P_c}{P_i} = \frac{\gamma^2}{(1-\gamma^1)}\frac{X_i^2}{X_c^1} \dots \dots \dots \dots \dots \quad (7)$$

$$P_c = 1 \quad \dots \dots \dots \dots \dots \dots \dots \quad (8)$$

Explanation

This model is simply an abbreviated form of the verbal explanation just given. Eq. (1) and (2) give the production points. Eq. (3) and (4) indicate what part of the production is to be consumed by the producer. Eq. (5) and (6) state that the demand is equal to the supply. Eq. (7) expresses the fact that the international price ratio is equal to the real terms of trade. Since country 2 retains the quantity $(1-\gamma^2)\,X_i^2$ for itself, it puts the quantity $\gamma^2\,X_i^2$ on the international market. Eq. (8) is the nominal price fixing basis. Substitution of the given values leads to the following confrontation table of resources and expenditure:

FREE TRADE, COMPLETE SPECIALIZATION

Country 1

Resources	Volume	Price	Value	Expend-iture	Volume	Price	Value
X_c^1	60	$\times\ 1$	$=\ 60$	S_c^1	30	$\times\ 1$	$=\ 30$
				S_i^1	40	$\times\ 0.75$	$=\ 30$
L^1	60	$\times\ 1$	$=\ 60$				60
Imports M_i^1	40	$\times\ 0.75$	$=\ 30$	Exports F_c^1	30	$\times\ 1$	$=\ 30$

Country 2

Resources	Volume	Price	Value	Expend-iture	Volume	Price	Value
X_i^2	80	$\times\ 0.75$	$=\ 60$	S_c^2	30	$\times\ 1$	$=\ 30$
				S_i^2	40	$\times\ 0.75$	$=\ 30$
L^2	80	$\times\ 0.75$	$=\ 60$				60
Imports M_c^2	30	$\times\ 1$	$=\ 30$	Exports F_i^2	40	$\times\ 0.75$	$=\ 30$

The ratio of the wage rates in both countries is so chosen as to give a rate of exchange of 1. Suppose the wage rate in country 2 was also 1, then P_i^2, the price of the I product in country 2, would amount to $\alpha_i^2\,P_L^2 = 1$. The price of the C product in country 1 is $P_c^1 = \alpha_c^1\,P_L^1 = 1$. On the international market, however, the price ratio is $P_i : P_c = 3 : 4$, from which it would follow that the exchange rate, i.e. the currency of country 2 in terms of the currency of country 1, would be $\frac{3}{4}$. To avoid these complications we choose the wage rate so as to make the rate of exchange equal to 1.

A comparison of the above confrontation tables with those on page 10 shows that country 1 and country 2 have both benefited from specialization and international trade. Eq. (7) demonstrates that the terms of trade are dependent (obviously) on supply and demand: the relative price of the C product will be higher the greater is the production of I ($= X_i^2$) and the smaller is the production of C ($= X_c^1$) and the greater the demand for C expressed in terms of γ^1 and γ^2.

INCOMPLETE SPECIALIZATION

Under complete specialization the international price ratio lies between the autarkic cost ratios of both countries. In the case discussed above, the international price ratio was greater than the cost ratio in country 2, but smaller than that in country 1. The international terms of trade, that in fact result, depend on supply and demand.

Given equal preferences for both countries, the supply ratio depends on the relative size of the two countries. The larger one country is than the other, the greater will be its supply and hence the less favourable its terms of trade. The limit to the deterioration of the terms of trade is reached as soon as the international price ratio is equal to the autarkic cost ratio in the large country. If the country were larger still, it would not have complete specialization. Specialization is pursued only until the exported quantity fetches a price, in terms of the imported product, equal to the domestic marginal ratio of substitution. The remaining demand for the imported product is then met by domestic production. The large country has nothing further to gain from international trade, because the imported product can be produced at the same costs at which it is now obtained by exchange.

It might be asked why country 2 still partly specializes if it does not in any case benefit from international trade. It should not be forgotten, however, that the situation described is one of equilibrium. Assuming that country 2 were to curtail its exports to country 1, then if the preferences remain the same the price of the exported product in terms of the imported product would rise and as a result it will again be advantageous for country 2 to specialize. Only in the state of equilibrium is there no advantage to be gained.

Incomplete specialization, as here described, might be called Graham's Case *.

Incomplete specialization can also be due, however, to the demand ratio, since of course the terms of trade are governed by supply *and* demand.

If the demand for the exported product of the small country is relatively small, the international terms of trade may be forced back to the autarkic cost ratio in the small country. If, therefore, in the above numerical example, the expenditure shares γ^1 and γ^2, for the exported product of the small country are not $\frac{1}{2}$ but only $\frac{1}{4}$, the international price ratio $\dfrac{P_i}{P_c} = \frac{1}{2}$ becomes equal to the autarkic cost ratio of the smaller country.

If there were even less propensity to spend on the C product, this country would be forced to abandon its complete specialization.

We may conclude from the foregoing that incomplete specialization is more probable than complete specialization (assuming linear transformation functions) the more the countries differ in size, the less is the demand for the product of the small country and the smaller are the relative cost differences.

The case of complete specialization, where the cost ratios were equal (page 7), was thus a special case because it can only occur where the sizes of the countries and of the expenditure shares stand in one specific relationship to one another.

Graphic Representation

The case of incomplete specialization can be illustrated with reference to fig. 3.

The production possibilities of country 1 are denoted by the

---

* F. D. Graham, The Theory of International Values Re-examined. *Quarterly Journal of Economics*, XXVIII (1923), p. 54-86. in: *Readings in the Theory of International Trade*, London (1950), p. 301-330.

line CD, those of country 2 by the line AB. The price ratio that would exist under autarky is indicated by the slope of CD and AB, respectively. Given the preference, we can thus construct the autarkic expenditure lines: OP and OQ. Now the price ratio $\dfrac{P_i^1}{P_c^1}$ is greater than $\dfrac{P_i^2}{P_c^2}$. This means that country 1 will specialize in the production of C. In accordance with the existing preference, this country will offer a part of its production, viz. ND, to its partner.

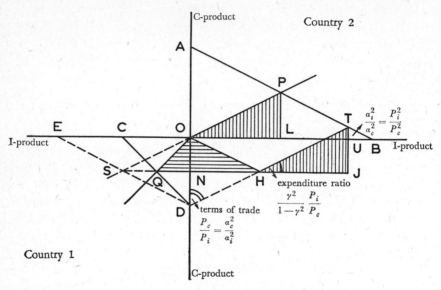

Figure 3. Incomplete specialization

Because of the relatively small supply of its own product it will be able to enjoy the most favourable terms of trade, which are equal to the autarkic price ratio in country 2. This determines the point H and the 'expenditure triangle' of country 1, i.e. ONH.

Unlike country 1, where the expenditure ratio is changed by free trade, in country 2 the expenditure ratio remains the same because the slope of the expenditure line $\left(\dfrac{\gamma^2}{1-\gamma^2} \cdot \dfrac{P_i^2}{P_c^2}\right)$ remains unchanged, the price ratios being identical under autarky and free trade. From point H we can now draw an expenditure line HT parallel to the original line OP. The production point T thus found shows that country 2 does not completely specialize. In addition to a quantity OU of the I product it makes a quantity UT of the C product.

From the foregoing it will be evident that country 2 has nothing to gain from free trade. The 'expenditure triangle' HJT is equal to the original triangle, OLP. Country 1, on the other hand, has profited considerably, as can be seen by comparing the triangle ONH = SNO with the original expenditure triangle QNO.

The above can again be briefly formulated in a set of equations.

Model 1.3 *Incomplete Specialization*

The model contains two production equations, three expenditure equations, one price equation and two equilibrium equations. With these eight equations we can solve the eight unknown variables, viz. three production volumes, four expenditure volumes and the price ratio.

$$X_c^1 = \frac{L^1}{\alpha_c^1} \qquad \qquad \text{(1)}$$

$$X_c^2 = \frac{L^2}{\alpha_c^2} - \frac{\alpha_i^2}{\alpha_c^2} X_i^2 \qquad \qquad \text{(2)}$$

$$S_c^1 = \gamma^1 X_c^1 \qquad \qquad \text{(3)}$$

$$S_c^1 = \frac{\gamma^1}{1 - \gamma^1} \frac{P_i}{P_c} S_i^1 \qquad \qquad \text{(4)}$$

$$S_c^2 = \frac{\gamma^2}{1 - \gamma^2} \frac{P_i}{P_c} S_i^2 \qquad \qquad \text{(5)}$$

$$\frac{P_i}{P_c} = \frac{\alpha_i^2}{\alpha_c^2} \qquad \qquad \text{(6)}$$

$$X_c^1 + X_c^2 = S_c^1 + S_c^2 \qquad \qquad \text{(7)}$$

$$X_i^2 = S_i^1 + S_i^2 \qquad \qquad \text{(8)}$$

Explanation

The production, eq. (1), and expenditure, eq. (3), of country 1, which specializes completely in one product, are established if the quantity of production factors, the technology and the preferences are given.

Eq. (2) gives the production possibilities of country 2. Eq. (4) and (5) indicate the desired expenditure ratios in country 1 and in country 2, respectively. Eq. (6) states that the international price ratio is equal to the cost ratio of country 2. Eq. (7) and (8) are equilibrium equations, equalizing supply and demand.

From eq. (1), (3), (4) and (6) the production and expenditure of country 1 can easily be found. Substitution of the values thus obtained, and of equations (2) and (5) in (7) and (8), gives two equations containing two unknowns. It seems unnecessary to elaborate on this somewhat lengthy discussion by providing a further numerical example.

CHAPTER II

INTERNATIONAL TRADE WITH
TWO SCARCE PRODUCTION FACTORS

In the foregoing it was assumed for the sake of simplicity that there was only one scarce factor, namely labour. We shall now widen the scope of the problem by assuming that both capital and labour are scarce production factors. We shall further assume that a certain substitution of capital and labour is possible, in that more than one technique can be applied per product. Capital can be replaced by labour (for the same production result) if a technique requiring a relatively high proportion of labour is substituted for one requiring a relatively high proportion of capital.

We shall again start from a two-country, two-product model and further, so as not to make the matter needlessly complicated, we shall confine ourselves to two techniques per product. The latter merely saves us calculation work, but imposes no essential restrictions on the validity of the model: the number of possible techniques can be extended ad libitum.

In the previous chapter the transformation curve was seen to be straight. The transformation curve can be defined as the locus of the maximum C production with a varying volume of I production. In the case we are now considering the transformation curve will not generally be straight, but will show a kink as often as a change-over is made to a different combination of techniques.

To make this clear we shall assume that the C product requires relatively more capital than the I product. If nothing but C is produced, maximum production can be achieved by choosing a combination of techniques which makes full use of the production factors. Since the C product has a high capital content, wide use will have to be made of a method of production requiring relatively more labour. If we now start to produce more I and less C, the necessary production factors for the I production will come not only from the curtailment of C production but also because in the

C production a larger proportion is produced by the method requiring relatively more capital: this is evident, since the I product requires more labour and less capital than becomes available through the reduced production of C.

This substitution process can only be continued, however, until the C commodity is produced solely by the method requiring more capital. If we want to continue substituting I for C, we must either introduce for the C product a technique requiring even more capital still, or a technique requiring more capital for the I product, or both. In any event the result will be a different substitution ratio for C and I. Graphically speaking this means that the transformation curve will show a kink. More kinks will appear the more techniques become relevant. In the case of an infinite number of techniques the transformation curve would be a flowing curve, progressively falling or, seen from the origin, concave in shape.

It would take us too far to deal comprehensively with the mathematical derivation of the transformation curve. This has already been done elsewhere *. It will be sufficient here, by way of transition from the straight to the curved transformation line, to treat graphically the intermediate case of the kinked transformation line for two techniques per commodity **.

TWO TECHNIQUES PER PRODUCT

The case of international trade where both capital and labour are scarce, and where the possibility of substituting these factors is limited to two techniques, is represented in fig. 4. The transformation lines are ARB and CSD, respectively. Under autarky the expenditure line (at $\gamma^2 = \frac{1}{2}$) will intersect the upper part of the transformation line of country 2 at the point P, which is thus the point of production and expenditure. At the given values (to be read from the coordinates in the figure) the price ratio is $\frac{P_i^2}{P_c^2} = \frac{1}{2}$, since the opportunity cost of the production of one

* See D. B. J. Schouten, *Exacte Economie*, Chapter 9.
**A similar case was dealt with in the article: Invoerrechten, inkomensverdeling en integratie, by D. B. J. Schouten (*Economie*, 1958, p. 5-30). There, however, the marginal substitution ratios of capital and labour were assumed to be equal, so that the transformation lines were again still straight lines.

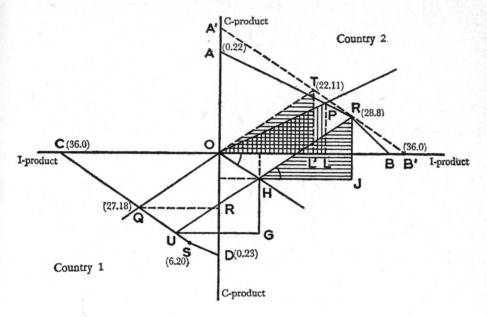

Figure 4. Free trade and autarky (two techniques per product)

more I product will amount to half a C product. This appears from the slope of the relevant line section AR. In country 1 the production and expenditure point Q (at $\gamma^1 = \frac{1}{2}$) lies on the section CS which has a slope of $\frac{2}{3}$, hence $\dfrac{P_i^1}{P_c^1} = \frac{2}{3}$. In the initial situation country 2 thus has an evident comparative advantage in the production of I. It will therefore specialize in this product, though not completely.

Suppose now that country 2 reduces its C production from 11 to 8 and raises its I production from 22 to 28; the production point is then shifted from P to R. At this point, however, the comparative advantage of country 2 ceases to exist. If it were to extend its I production still further, the production costs of I in terms of C would rise from $\frac{1}{2}$ to 1 (since the section RB has a slope equal to 1) whilst country 1 would at the most be prepared to offer $\frac{2}{3}$ of a C product for one I product. At point R then, the specialization of country 2 will come to a halt.

The equilibrium terms of trade will then be equal to the substitution ratio of C and I in country 1, that is $\dfrac{P_i}{P_c} = \frac{2}{3}$, for country 1 cannot accept higher terms of trade because it has a better alternative. Under lower terms of trade, country 1 would continue substituting C for I, although there is no market to be found for this surplus C product. The equilibrium terms of trade must therefore be $\frac{2}{3}$.

Equilibrium on the international market can be construed graphically as follows: the line representing the terms of trade (OH) has a slope of $\frac{2}{3}$, equal to the cost ratio in country 1. The expenditure line of country 2 has a slope of $\dfrac{\gamma^2}{1-\gamma^2} \cdot \dfrac{P_i}{P_c} = \frac{2}{3}$. If we now draw this expenditure line from the point R, the point (H) where this line intersects the terms of trade line is the point of international trade. The expenditure line of country 1 must also have a slope of $\frac{2}{3}$. If we draw this line from the point H, the point (U) where it intersects the transformation line is the production point of country 1. The quantity HK of C product is exchanged for a quantity OK of I product.

Comparison of the 'expenditure triangle' UGH with QNO, and of HJR = OL'T with OLP, shows that, as expected, country 2 derives advantage from international trade, whereas country 1 neither gains nor loses by it.

It will be clear from the above that, on the given assumptions of scarce capital and labour and the possibility of substituting one for the other, there is little opportunity for complete specialization. This is feasible only if the cost ratio in the one country is smaller on all sections of the transformation line than the lowest cost ratio in the other country.

CURVED TRANSFORMATION LINES AND
INDIFFERENCE CURVES

The assumption of a limited number of techniques per product, although certainly not unrealistic, is not frequently made in the theory of international trade. Most authors adopt curved transformation lines, thereby assuming, at least implicitly, an infinite number of techniques per product.

In fig. 5 an attempt is made to show the relation between the line of thought followed by these authors * and our own approach to the problem.

The transformation lines AB and CD are curved lines. Regarding the demand side we have assumed a fixed expenditure share of income, whereas the authors work on a system of indifference curves. The relation between our assumption and the system of indifference curves resides in the fact that where the expenditure shares are fixed the elasticity of substitution of demand, which is a measure of the curvature of the indifference curves, amounts to 1. This is of course an arbitrary assumption, but is it any more so than one or another arbitrarily drawn system of indifference curves?

Moreover, it is not essential to our approach to assume fixed expenditure shares, since we can let them vary with the price ratio if the elasticity of substitution of demand is put at a higher value. This will be done in the following chapters.

Under autarky the production and expenditure point will be where the transformation curve is tangent to an indifference curve, for at that point the welfare index will be highest. If, however, the slopes of the lines tangent both to the transformation curve and to the indifference curve are not the same in both countries, it will then be advantageous to enter into international trade. To avoid overburdening the graph, the lines tangent to the autarkic equilibrium points are not drawn. Nevertheless, it is evident that the tangent at P has a smaller slope than the tangent at Q. This means that in country 1 the C product in terms of the I product is cheaper than in country 2, and conversely in country 2 the I product is relatively cheaper than in country 1.

* See F. de Roos, *Inleiding tot de theorie der internationale economische betrekkingen,* Haarlem 1957, page 56 ff. and the works there referred to.

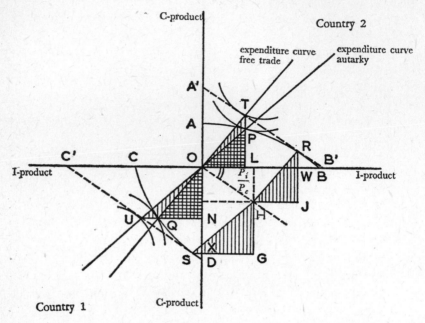

Figure 5. Expenditure under free trade and under autarky
(curved transformation functions)

Country 2 will thus produce more of the I product and country 1 more of the C product. The production point in country 2 thus moves lower down the transformation curve. The same takes place in country 2. The equilibrium point found must now meet two conditions:

a. The cost ratio must be the same in both countries, i.e. the slope of the line tangent to the transformation curve must be the same at the production point of country 1 as at the production point of country 2.

b. The total supply must correspond to the total demand.

The significance of this second condition may be explained as follows. It is possible to draw an infinite number of tangents to the two transformation curves, that all have the same slope. These all meet the first condition, but not all of them meet the second. All these tangents also touch an indifference curve. The point where they do so will be eligible as an expenditure point, because welfare is greatest at that point. Now, amongst the infinite pairs of tangents there is only one pair whose points of contact on the indifference curves represent expenditure points such that the total expenditure is equal to the total production.

Fig. 5 gives an idea of the equilibrium situation envisaged here. The tangents A'B' and C'D' have the same slope, so that the first condition is satisfied. These tangents touch indifference curves at T and U, respectively. Now the total expenditure is equal to the total production. The 'expenditure triangles' HJR and SGH, which are equal to OLT and UNO, respectively, make this quite clear. Country 2 consumes an amount RJ of the C commodity, of which the portion RW is produced at home and the portion WJ = LH is imported. The remainder of the quantity of C produced is consumed by country 1. Country 1 consumes SG of the I commodity, of which the portion SX is produced at home whilst XG = OL is imported. The remainder of the I production is consumed by country 2.

The tangent $\dfrac{HL}{OL}$ gives the international terms of trade $\dfrac{P_i}{P_c}$. The angle HOL is equal to the angle A'B'O and to D'C'O, which again satisfies the condition that the international price ratio must be equal to the cost ratio of the products in both countries.

Synopsis

We can now draw a comparison between figures 3, 4 and 5. Although the assumptions in the three cases are different, they amount to the same thing in principle. In the autarkic situation the price ratio is such as to give rise to specialization. In the equilibrium situation the international terms of trade are equal to 'the' marginal substitution ratio of C and I: the lines C'D' (in fig. 4 CD), OH and A'B' (in fig. 3 AB) are parallel to one another. The difference, however, is that in fig. 5 the equilibrium comes about because in *both* countries the marginal substitution ratios of C and I are equal, whereas in fig. 3 and fig. 4 the equilibrium arises because country 1 and country 2, respectively, gain the maximum advantage, whilst the partner must be content with an international price ratio equal to the autarkic terms of exchange, i.e. its marginal ratio of substitution.

In the last two cases international trade is therefore advantageous only to one of the partners. One might supplement the parallel between the figures by drawing at points Q and Q' in fig. 3 indifference curves tangent to CD and C'D, respectively. It is then plain that in at least one of the two countries the expenditure points in international trade lie on a higher indifference curve than the expenditure in the case of autarky.

ECONOMIES OF SCALE

In the foregoing we have seen that, given equal preferences, international trade is advantageous only where the ratio of costs is different in the countries concerned.

A case is conceivable, however, given identical technologies in two countries with identical preferences and costs structure, where international trade and an increase in specialization yield an advantage for both countries. This case arises where 'economies of scale' exist. Many authors dealing with the subject of integration therefore lay considerable emphasis on the increase of productivity which will result from a wider market. It will then be possible to apply techniques that demand a wide sales outlet. The quantities produced by mass production can be increased, thereby reducing the cost. *

In terms of our foregoing considerations, economies of scale mean that the transformation line, seen from the origin, becomes convex. If, as indicated in fig. 6, a country starts to specialize from point P, and for example, begins producing more I commodities with the same means of production, the cost of the I commodity will fall and that of the C commodity will rise. What are the consequences of this for international trade?

To answer this question we assume that two countries have the

---

* See: P. J. Verdoorn, *Prae-advies voor de Vereniging voor de Staathuishoudkunde*, The Hague, 1952, pp. 54-57.

same means of production, and also that their technologies and preferences are identical ($\gamma^1 = \gamma^2 = \frac{1}{2}$). We have seen above that if the transformation functions were linear, international trade would yield no advantage. Now, however, it does, as appears from fig. 6.

The first quadrant contains the production and expenditure point P, which applies in the case of autarky. In the third quadrant this point is indicated by Q. Since we have started from completely identical data, the price ratio in both countries is equal: $P_c^1 : P_i^1 = P_c^2 : P_i^2$. The price ratio is determined by the marginal substitution ratio of C and I, or by the number of C products that must be forgone in order to make one I product more; expressed as a formula $\dfrac{P_i}{P_c} = -\dfrac{dC}{dI}$. This differential quotient is simply the slope of the line tangent to a particular point on the transformation curve.

In the initial situation neither country has any comparative advantage in producing any commodity. The situation changes as soon as, for example, country 2 starts to produce somewhat more of the I commodity. The production point shifts to the right, and the tangent to the transformation curve acquires a smaller slope, which means that the price ratio $\dfrac{P_i^2}{P_c^2}$ becomes smaller. Country 2 now has a comparative advantage in producing I, and this advantage will be greater the more country 1 specializes in the production of C.

There is no reason at all, however, why country 2 should specialize in I production, because if it specializes in C production it will achieve the same result, provided country 1 then applies itself to the production of I.

Let us assume that country 2 embarks exclusively on I production, and produces a quantity OB. Country 1 produces OD. In accordance with the existing preferences the resultant terms of trade will be those described in the preceding chapter (page 8). The expenditure after specialization can be read from the hatched 'expenditure triangles' in the fourth quadrant which, transferred to the first and third quadrants, are evidently larger than the original 'expenditure triangles'. Under autarky the 'expenditure triangle' of country 2 is OLP and of country 1 QNO. Under com-

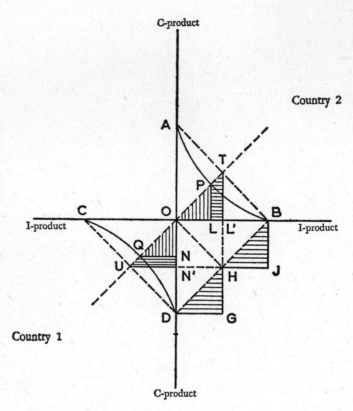

Figure 6. International trade and economies of scale

plete specialization and international trade they are OL'T and UN'O, respectively, which correspond to HJB and DGH.

The remarkable point about the case envisaged here is that, in the initial situation, there is no comparative cost advantage, notwithstanding the fact that specialization is shown to be advantageous to both parties. It is indeed the specialization that *creates* the comparative advantage. The big question here, however, is which country is going to specialize in the production of I commodities and which in C commodities. It may of course be answered that this depends on the outlook of the entrepreneurs. If the entrepreneurs in the one country specialize in I production, those in the other country will specialize in C production.

Where, however, for political reasons, both countries specialize in the same product, considerable wastage results. Mutual agreements, or perhaps even a supranational form of control, will then be necessary to obtain an optimum result.

CHAPTER III

THE SIGNIFICANCE OF IMPORT
DUTIES UNDER COMPLETE SPECIALIZATION

Before discussing the customs union, i.e. the abolition of import duties, we shall consider the effect which the imposition of an import duty has on international trade. This has didactic as well as logical advantages. In a customs union there are always at least three parties involved: the two countries that enter into the union and the outsiders. The problem therefore calls for at least a three-country model, whereas the consequences of levying an import duty can very clearly be illustrated with a much simpler two-country model.

Assumptions

In examining the effect of import duties on international trade we shall take as our first starting point a two-country, two-product model. Country 1 is entirely specialized in C production and country 2 in I production. The data for the initial situation are set out in the following confrontation tables of resources and expenditure.

FREE TRADE

Country 1

Resources	Volume	Price	Value	Expenditure	Volume	Price	Value
X_c^1	200	$\times$ 1	= 200	S_c^1	100	$\times$ 1	= 100
				S_i^1	100	$\times$ 1	= 100
			— 200				— 200
Imports				Exports			
M_i^1	100	$\times$ 1	= 100	F_c^1	100	$\times$ 1	= 100

Country 2

Resources	Volume	Price	Value	Expend- iture	Volume	Price	Value
X_i^2	200	× 1	= 200	S_c^2	100	× 1	= 100
				S_i^2	100	× 1	= 100
			200				200
Imports				Exports			
M_c^2	100	× 1	= 100	F_i^2	100	× 1	= 100

We further assume that all direct elasticities of demand are equal to —1, the indirect elasticities of demand to 0 and the income elasticities of demand to +1. The elasticities of demand are denoted by the letter η, provided with two subscripts, the prefix indicating the commodity whose price varies, and the suffix the commodity whose volume varies. For example, $_c\eta_c$ is the direct elasticity of demand for the C product and $_i\eta_c$ the indirect elasticity of demand for the C product in relation to changes in the price of the I commodity. The income elasticity is denoted by the letter μ.

On the supply side we shall provisionally assume complete inelasticity, in other words we suppose that the supply remains unchanged and that there is full employment in the initial and final situations.

Import Duties

Suppose now that country 1 imposes a duty on the I commodity imported from country 2. What changes will this give rise to in the prices and volumes, assuming there must be equilibrium in the balance of payments?

In the first instance we have merely one price change, namely p_i^1, i.e. the price of the I commodity on the home market of country 1.

As a result of this increase in price and of the effect which the revenue from the import duty has on income, the demand for C commodities in country 1 will rise. The demand for I commodities will fall owing to their higher price, but the fall will be mitigated by the positive effect which the revenue from the import duty has had on national income. In the first instance nothing has happened in country 2, and therefore the general equilibrium has been disturbed. To restore equilibrium, i.e. to ensure that the total demand for C products will again fall and the demand for I products rises again, the price of the C product compared with that of the I product will have to be adopted. This means that corrective measures will have to be adopted. For our purpose it is not material whether these measures relate to devaluation of the currency of country 2, revaluation of the currency of country 1, deflation of wages and prices in country 2 or inflation of wages and prices in country 1; what we are concerned with are the changes in the *price ratio*. As the instrument adopted to restore equilibrium we shall choose the price of the product of country 1, i.e. P_c^1, whilst the price P_i^2 will be kept constant.

We can now solve the problem with the aid of a two-phase model or with a simultaneous model, which amounts to the same thing.

TWO-PHASE MODEL

Model 3.1   First phase

$$\Delta S_c^1 = S_c^1 s_c^1 \quad \dots \dots \dots \dots \dots \dots \quad (1)$$

$$s_c^1 = {}_c\eta_c^1 p_c^1 + {}_i\eta_c^1 p_i^1 + \mu q_m^1 t_i^1 \quad \dots \dots \dots \dots \quad (2)$$

$$\Delta S_i^1 = S_i^1 s_i^1 \quad \dots \dots \dots \dots \dots \dots \quad (3)$$

$$s_i^1 = {}_c\eta_i^1 p_c^1 + {}_i\eta_i^1 p_i^1 + \mu q_m^1 t_i^1 \quad \dots \dots \dots \dots \quad (4)$$

$$p_c^1 = 0 \quad \dots \dots \dots \dots \dots \dots \dots \quad (5)$$

$$p_i^1 = t_i^1 \quad \dots \dots \dots \dots \dots \dots \dots \quad (6)$$

Explanation

The absolute quantities are denoted by capital letters, the relative deviations from the initial values by small letters. For example,

$$s_c^1 = \frac{\Delta S_c^1}{S_c^1}, \quad p_c^1 = \frac{\Delta P_c^1}{P_c^1}.$$

The absolute change of the volume of expenditure is equal to the product of the initial volume and its relative change. The relative change is a function of the price changes and of the changes in income *. We assume that the government spends the revenue from the import duty, possibly by way of a tax reduction, in accordance with the same preferences as in the national economy as a whole. We therefore assume that the income elasticity of demand for all commodities is equal to the average income elasticity, namely 1. The effect on income is that the volume of the expenditure on the various commodities increases by the same percentage as income. The percentage increase of income due to revenue from import duties is equal to the import share multiplied by the ad valorem tariff. The import share is that proportion of the value of the national expenditure represented by the value of the imports. It is evident that if the import duty is $t_i^1 = 20\%$ and the imports amount to half the national expenditure, $q_m^1 = 0.5$, the revenue from the import duty will be 0.5 × 20% of the national expenditure. The import share is denoted by the symbol q_m, the suffix m serving to distinguish the import share from the expenditure share q_s and the production share q_x, which will be dealt with later.

It is now a simple matter, with the aid of model 3.1, to calculate the changes in the expenditures S_c^1 and S_i^1. However, since the production of the C commodity in country 1 remains unchanged, an increase in real expenditure on the C product implies a drop in exports, and since country 1 does not produce the I commodity, a decrease in expenditure on the I commodity implies a drop in imports. This is the primary effect of imposing an import duty. There being no occasion in the first instance for country 2 to make any change in its expenditure, the prices, like the income, remain unchanged, so that this primary effect constitutes a disturbance of the general equilibrium: the total demand for the C commodity is greater and the total demand for the I commodity is smaller than the total supply.

In the second phase the equilibrium will have to be restored by an increase in the price of the C commodity in relation to the price of the I commodity. In other words,

---

* The revenue from an import duty is merely a nominal increment of income, and is exactly compensated by the nominal increase in expenditure as a result of the higher prices of the imported commodity.

The disturbed equilibrium on the international market must be restored by improving the terms of trade of the country imposing the import duty. This is done in model 3.2.

Model 3.2   Second Phase

$$\Delta S_c + S_c^1 s_c^1 + S_c^2 s_c^2 = 0 \quad \ldots \ldots \ldots \ldots \ldots \ldots (1)$$

$$s_c^1 = {}_c\eta_c^1 p_c + {}_i\eta_c^1 p_i + \mu\, p_c \quad \ldots \ldots \ldots \ldots (2)$$

$$s_c^2 = {}_c\eta_c^2 p_c + {}_i\eta_c^2 p_i \quad \ldots \ldots \ldots \ldots \ldots (3)$$

$$p_i = 0 \quad \ldots \ldots \ldots \ldots \ldots \ldots \ldots \ldots (4)$$

Explanation

Since the C production remains unchanged, equilibrium will prevail only where the sum of the changes in real expenditure is equal to zero. As stated above, we have chosen as the instrument for creating equilibrium the export price of the country that imposes the import duty; this has the advantage that it immediately shows the improvement of the terms of trade of that country. In equation (1) the first term ΔS_c, that is the change in the demand for C products resulting from the first phase, is a known quantity, whilst the second and third terms may be expressed in P_c. In equation (2) we find an income effect in addition to the price effects. The increase in the price by a certain percentage increases the income from production by the same percentage. This higher income causes, via the income elasticity μ, an increase in real expenditure. By substitution we can calculate the relative and absolute changes in expenditure and thus in the imports and exports of the C commodity. Finally, summation of the changes resulting from the first and second phases gives the ultimate change in the import and export of the C commodity.

The change in the import and export of the I commodity can now be calculated quite simply, since the change in the terms of trade which brings the demand for the C product into line with the supply, automatically creates equilibrium between the supply and demand in respect of the I product. This can be proved as follows. * If there is equilibrium in the balance of payments ** and if the demand for the C product is in equilibrium with the

* The proof given here is formulated in the most general sense so as to include the case of incomplete specialization.
**We shall distinguish between balance of trade and balance of payments only where the context requires it.

supply, then the demand for the I product is also in equilibrium with the supply, equilibrium in the balance of payments being symbolized as follows:

$$(S_i^1 - X_i^1)\, P_i = (X_c^1 - S_c^1)\, P_c \quad \dots \quad \dots \quad (5)$$

$$(S_c^2 - X_c^2)\, P_c = (X_i^2 - S_i^2)\, P_i \quad \dots \quad \dots \quad (6)$$

The volume of imports is equal to the volume of expenditure minus domestic production, just as exports are equal to domestic production minus the volume of expenditure. Summation and regrouping of equations (5) and (6) gives;

$$(S_i^1 + S_i^2 - X_i^1 - X_i^2)\, P_i = - (S_c^1 + S_c^2 - X_c^1 - X_c^2)\, P_c \; . \quad (7)$$

If supply and demand in respect of the C product are in equilibrium then the right-hand side of equation (7) is equal to zero, from which it follows that the supply and demand in respect of the I product are also equal to one another.

We must now prove that our equations imply equilibrium in the balance of payments. This is not difficult if we remember that equilibrium in the balance of payments is an expression of the equality of income and (money) expenditure.

The income elasticity, $\mu = 1$, which is consistently applied to all income effects * guarantees that in our model the whole of the income will be spent, or at least the increase of income (where the balance of payments is not in equilibrium in the initial situation) and not more than the increase of income.

The term income elasticity, as used here, is more a theoretical concept than an empirical quantity. Amongst the empirically found income elasticities, some are greater than unity ands others smaller than unity. The postulate that the average income elasticity must be equal to unity is based on the theoretical view that, over a somewhat longer term, Say's law must apply and that therefore the expenditure must be equal to income, in so far as the government's financial policy is a sound one. We make the latter assumption in all cases, and therefore we assume also that the revenue from the import duty will lead to a tax reduction, just as the abolition of the import duty is compensated by higher taxation.

---

* See appendix 1, where it is shown that the real effect on income of the price changes is included in the elasticities of demand.

SIMULTANEOUS MODEL

Although we prefer the two-phase model in view of its greater clarity, we shall nevertheless give the simultaneous model, which amounts essentially to the same thing.

Model 3.3   Imposition of Import Duty, Complete Specialization

$$S_c^1 s_c^1 + S_c^2 s_c^2 = 0 \quad \ldots \ldots \ldots \ldots \ldots \ldots \quad (1)$$

$$s_c^1 = {}_c\eta_c^1 p_c^1 + {}_i\eta_c^1 p_i^1 + \mu (p_c^1 + q_m^1 t_i^1) \quad \ldots \ldots \ldots \quad (2)$$

$$s_c^2 = {}_c\eta_c^2 p_c^2 + {}_i\mu_c^2 p_i^2 \quad \ldots \ldots \ldots \ldots \ldots \quad (3)$$

$$p_i^1 = p_i^2 + t_i^1 \quad \ldots \ldots \ldots \ldots \ldots \ldots \quad (4)$$

$$p_i^2 = 0 \quad \ldots \ldots \ldots \ldots \ldots \ldots \ldots \quad (5)$$

$$p_c^1 = p_c^2 \quad \ldots \ldots \ldots \ldots \ldots \ldots \ldots \quad (6)$$

Explanation

Since the change in C production is zero, the change in C expenditure must also on balance be zero. This is expressed in equation (1). The percentage change of C expenditure in country 1 depends on the price changes, that is to say on the change of P_i, which increases with the import duty, and on the change of P_c, which is the change in the terms of trade designed to create equilibrium; it depends also on the change in income, which consists in an increased value of production and in the revenue from the import duty. In country 2 there is no effect on income. Once the change in the terms of trade is known, the percentage change in the expenditure on I in country 1 can be calculated from the formula

$$s_i^1 = {}_c\eta_i^1 p_c^1 + {}_i\eta_i^1 p_i^1 + \mu (p_c^1 + q_m^1 t_i^1)$$

and in country 2 from the formula

$$s_i^2 = {}_c\eta_i^2 p_c^2 + {}_i\eta_i^2 p_i^2$$

The simultaneous model leads to the same solution as the two-phase model.

Numerical Example

The tariff imposed amounts to 20 % ad valorem. We further assume that the direct elasticities of demand are —1 and the indirect 0. Substitution of the assumed data (see page 30-31) in model 3.1 gives:

$$\Delta S_c^1 = 100 s_c^1 \quad \ldots \ldots \ldots \ldots \ldots \ldots \ldots \quad (1)$$

$$s_c^1 = -1 \times 0 + 0 \times 0.20 + 0.5 \times 0.20 \quad \ldots \ldots \ldots \quad (2)$$

$$\Delta S_i^1 = 100 \, s_i^1 \, . \quad . \quad . \quad . \quad . \quad . \quad . \quad . \quad . \quad . \quad . \quad . \quad . \quad . \quad . \quad . \quad . \quad . \quad (3)$$

$$s_i^1 = 0 \times 0 - 1 \times 0.20 + 0.5 \times 0.20 \quad . \quad . \quad . \quad . \quad . \quad . \quad . \quad (4)$$

From this it follows in the first instance that $\Delta S_c^1 = +10$ and $\Delta S_i^1 = -10$. Substitution of the change thus found and of the data in model 3.2 gives:

$$10 + 100 \, s_c^1 + 100 \, s_c^2 = 0 \quad . \quad . \quad . \quad . \quad . \quad . \quad . \quad . \quad . \quad . \quad . \quad (1)$$

$$s_c^1 = -1 \, p_c + 0 \times 0 + p_c \quad . \quad . \quad . \quad . \quad . \quad . \quad . \quad . \quad . \quad (2)$$

$$s_c^2 = -1 \, p_c + 0 \times 0 \, . \quad . \quad . \quad . \quad . \quad . \quad . \quad . \quad . \quad . \quad . \quad (3)$$

Hence $P_c = 0.10$. The reduced demand for the C product owing to the price increase is thus in the second instance exactly compensated in country 1 by the increased demand due to the effect on income. In the second phase, then, the expenditure on C remains unchanged. In country 2 the expenditure on C decreases by 10, so that summation of the results of the first and second phases shows that supply and demand for the C product are in equilibrium.

With the calculated price change p_c we can now also calculate the change in the expenditure on I. For country 1 this change is:

$$\Delta S_i^1 = S_i^1 \, s_i^1,$$

and we have:

$$s_i^1 = {}_c \eta_i^1 \, p_c + {}_i \eta_i^1 \, p_i + \mu \, p_c = 0.10.$$

The I expenditure of country 1 thus increases in the second phase by 10. For country 2 we have:

$$\Delta S_i^2 = S_i^2 \, s_i^2, \text{ where } s_i^2 = {}_c \eta_i^2 \, p_c + {}_i \eta_i^2 \, p_i = 0.$$

Supply and demand in respect of the I product are therefore also in equilibrium.

We can now set these results out in a confrontation table of the changes in resources and expenditure.

CHANGES DUE TO IMPOSITION
OF 20 % IMPORT DUTY ON THE I COMMODITY

Country 1

Re-sources	Δ Volume	Δ Price	Δ Value	Expend-iture	Δ Volume	Δ Price	Δ Value
X_c^1	$200 \times 0 + 200 \times 0.1$		$= 20$	S_c^1	$100 \times 0.1 + 100 \times 0.1$		$= 20$
T_i^1		100×0.2	$= 20$	S_i^1	100×0	$+ 100 \times 0.2$	$= 20$
			$\overline{}$ 40				$\overline{}$ 40
Imports M_i^1	$100 \times 0 + 100 \times 0$		$= 0$	Exports F_c^1	$100 \times -0.1 + 100 \times 0.1$		$= 0$

Country 2

Re-sources	Δ Volume	Δ Price	Δ Value	Expend-iture	Δ Volume	Δ Price	Δ Value
X_i^2	$200 \times 0 + 200 \times 0$		$= 0$	S_c^2	$100 \times -0.1 + 100 \times 0.1$		$= 0$
				S_i^2	100×0	$+ 100 \times 0$	$= 0$
			$\overline{}$ 0				$\overline{}$ 0
Imports M_c^2	$100 \times -0.1 + 100 \times 0.1$		$= 0$	Exports F_i^2	100×0	$+ 100 \times 0$	$= 0$

In drawing up the confrontation of changes in resources and expenditure we assume that, *in approximation*, the sum of the change in value due to the change in volume, given constant prices, and the change in value due to the change in price, given constant volume, is equal to the total change in value. The second-order effect is thus disregarded here.

Retaliatory Tariffs

We have seen that, in the given assumptions, country 1 has improved its terms of trade by 10 % in that it has acquired 10 % more C products at the expense of country 2. Country 2, however, will not fail to react and will take measures of retaliation. To simplify the situation mathematically, we can consider what will happen if both countries at the same time (not successively) impose an import duty of 20 % ($t_i^1 = t_c^2 = 0.2$). The result is: $p_c^1 = 0$; $\Delta S_c^2 = \Delta M_c^2 = -10$; $\Delta S_i^1 = \Delta M_i^1 = -10$.

The final situation for country 1 can be represented in a confrontation table as follows:

CHANGES WHERE BOTH
COUNTRIES IMPOSE A 20 % IMPORT DUTY

Country 1

Resources	Δ Volume	Δ Price	Δ Value	Expend-iture	Δ Volume	Δ Price	Δ Value
X_c^1	0 + 0		= 0	S_c^1	10 + 0		= 10
T_i^1			20	S_i^1	−10 + 20		= 10
			— 20				— 20
Imports			=	Exports			=
M_i^1	−10 + 0		= −10	F_c^1	−10 + 0		= −10

The same confrontation applies mutatis mutandis to country 2.

CONCLUSION

It appears from the foregoing that the only result of the tariff imposition is a decline in international trade. Each country consumes 10 % more of its own product and 10% less of the imported product. General welfare calculated with the old prices as index, has not changed, but only the pattern of expenditure. In the given circumstances the tariff is rather pointless, just as, if the initial situation corresponded to our final situation, the abolition of import duties would promote international trade but not general welfare. The 'given circumstances' are, however, very specific, so that this conclusion calls for some qualification (see page 43).

PROHIBITIVE IMPORT DUTIES

Definition

The consequences of imposing (and abolishing) import duties may be much more serious than the previous case suggests, namely where prohibitive import duties are imposed. Suppose that country 1 can also produce I commodities, but 10 % dearer than country 2, and that country 2 can also produce C commodities, but 10 % dearer than country 1. The cost ratios are then:

$$\frac{P_c^1}{P_i^1} = \frac{1}{1.1} \text{ and } \frac{P_c^2}{P_i^2} = \frac{1.1}{1}.$$

The comparative difference in costs has led to complete specialization. If import duties higher than 20 % are now imposed, the comparative difference of costs will be eliminated, the price ratio $\frac{P_c^1}{P_i^1}$ in country 1 will become greater than $\frac{1}{1.1}$ and country 1 will thus itself embark on the production of the imported commodity. In concrete terms, the importers will be driven off the market by the competition offered by home production. In this case one speaks of prohibitive import duties.

Numerical Example

To illustrate the consequences of a prohibitive import duty, we shall specify somewhat the numerical example given in the previous sections. Labour is the scarce production factor, the available quantity of which amounting to 200 in both countries: $L^1 = L^2 = 200$. The technologies are expressed by the labour inputs per unit of product:

$$\alpha_c^1 = 1 \qquad \alpha_c^2 = 1.1$$
$$\alpha_i^1 = 1.1 \qquad \alpha_i^2 = 1.$$

Furthermore, the wage rate in both countries is equal to unity and the expenditure share for the C commodity is $\gamma = \frac{1}{2}$.

Given these data in the case of free trade, complete specialization will arise and the final situation is represented in the confrontation tables on page 30—31. Suppose now that in country 1 an import duty of 30 % is imposed on the I commodity. It will then be more advantageous for this country to revert to the autarkic position. International trade comes to a halt, and country 2 also is forced to produce its own C product. The new situation of equilibrium can be calculated by inserting the above data in the autarkic model 1.1 (page 4). Disregarding secondary effects, the new confrontation for country 1 will now be as follows:

PROHIBITIVE IMPORT DUTY

Country 1

Resources	Volume	Price	Value	Expend-iture	Volume	Price	Value
X_c^1	100	× 1	= 100	S_c^1	100	× 1	= 100
X_i^1	90	× 1.1	= 100	S_i^1	90	× 1.1	= 100
			200				200

Imports and exports have stopped completely. National welfare, too, has appreciably declined. If we compare this confrontation with that on page 30, we see that, given the same consumption of C, the real expenditure on I has dropped by 10 %.

The magnitude of this loss of welfare can be calculated as the product of the difference in (labour) costs and the reduction of international trade. This, then, is the amount of labour that can be saved by importing certain commodities instead of producing them oneself.

In our example this means for country 1: $(\alpha_i^1 - \alpha_i^2) \times \Delta M_i^1 =$

$(1.1-1) \times (-100) = -10$. This conclusion is only valid, however, where *prohibitive* import duties are concerned.

Under complete specialization prohibitive import duties do not leave specialization and total welfare unaffected

IMPROVEMENT OF THE TERMS OF TRADE

If no foreign measures of retaliation are taken, a country can improve its terms of trade by imposing import duties, as long as they are not prohibitive. From the confrontation on page 38 it appears that, in the given numerical example, the real exports of the C product from country 1 decrease by 10 % where the imports of I goods remain unchanged. The terms of trade in the case of free trade amounted to 100 C products for 100 I goods, or $\dfrac{P_c}{P_i} = 1$, whilst after imposing a 20 % import duty the terms of trade were $\dfrac{100}{90}$, representing an improvement of 10 %. A higher import duty will improve the terms of trade still further, a lower import duty less. The improvement in the terms of trade, however, depends not only on how high the import duty is, but also on the import value share (which in case of equilibrium in the balance of payments equals the export value share). The fact that this is so appears from the simultaneous model 3.3 on page 36. The percentage change in the terms of trade of country 1 is indicated in this model by p_c^1, since the price level in the outside world is assumed to be constant ($p_i^2 = 0$). Substitution of the equations (2) to (6) in (1) gives:

$$p_c^1 = \frac{S_c^1}{S_c^2}\, q_{mi}^1\, t_i^1 = (1 - q_{mi}^1)\, t_i^1. *$$

The improvement in the terms of trade will thus be greater the higher the duty imposed and the smaller the value share of imports of the country imposing the duty.

* $\dfrac{S_c^1}{S_c^2} = \dfrac{X_c^1 - S_c^2}{S_c^2} = \dfrac{1}{q_{mi}} - 1$ if the export share $\dfrac{S_c^2\, P_c}{X_c^1\, P_c}$ equals the import share q_{mi}.

If, however, a foreign retaliatory tariff has been imposed, the improvement in the terms of trade is then:

$$p_c^1 = (1 - q_{mi}^1) \, t_i^1 - (1 - q_{mc}^2) \, t_c^2.$$

It follows that, under the given elasticities, the improvement in country 1's terms of trade will be smaller the higher the retaliatory tariff and the smaller the import share in country 2.

The above shows that the conclusion on page 40, that the simultaneous imposition of an import duty does not change the level of welfare (in this case the terms of trade) is valid only if the countries are roughly identical in size and in demand structure.

THE LIMIT TO THE IMPROVEMENT OF THE TERMS OF TRADE

There must obviously be a limit to the improvement possible in the terms of trade. The limit is reached as soon as the import duty becomes prohibitive. It may become prohibitive in two ways, however. It may be because, in the country imposing the duty, the ratio of the price of the imported product to that of the exported product becomes higher than the autarkic cost ratio of both goods. This point has already been touched on (cf. page 40).

The tariff may also, however, become prohibitive to the partner country's imports, since an improvement in the terms of trade of country 1 means a worsening of the terms of trade of country 2. This change is subject to the same limits as the change in the domestic price ratio in country 1 : trade ceases as soon as one of the countries on the international market must forgo more I products to obtain one C product than it would have to forgo to make this C product itself.

CHAPTER IV

THE SIGNIFICANCE
OF IMPORT DUTIES UNDER INCOMPLETE
INTERNATIONAL SPECIALIZATION

Supply Functions in International Trade

In discussing the effect of import duties on international trade we have hitherto confined ourselves to the demand functions: we assumed a given supply, which in fact implied complete specialization. We therefore found that import duties, although influencing the volume of international trade and being capable of altering the terms of trade, nevertheless have no effect on the structure of production, unless the import duty is prohibitive.

We shall now include the supply factors explicitly in our considerations. In the first and second chapters we have already considered various supply curves, as the transformation lines may also be called. Where there is one scarce production factor the transformation curve is a straight line. Where there are two scarce production factors, however, and two techniques per product, we obtain a bent transformation curve which, in certain cases, i.e. where the slopes of the isoquanta of both products are equal, again becomes a straight line (page 20). When there are more than two techniques per product, the number of kinks in the curve may increase, and with an infinite number of techniques per product the transformation curve becomes a flowing line which can also, however, become a straight line in certain circumstances (where the curvature of the isoquanta is identical). The latter will be the case, for example, if the production functions of the C product and of the I product are Cobb-Douglas production functions of the form: $C = L^\alpha K^{1-\alpha}$ and $I = L^\alpha K^{1-\alpha}$. But this is a very special case, and the transformation functions will therefore generally be curved lines. Disregarding economies of scale (page 26) these curves will slope progressively downwards (concave seen from the origin). We shall now try to incorporate these curved supply functions into the theory of general equilibrium. We confine ourselves first of all to a closed economy.

CLOSED ECONOMY

If we are to include the supply function in a model and a numerical example, we must make a certain assumption in regard to the form of this function. Since the usefulness of a numerical example lies more in its ease of manipulation than in its realism, we shall assume our supply function to be a circle.

Model 4.1 *Closed Economy*

Equilibrium in a closed economy can be represented in a model as follows:

$$(C)^2 + (I)^2 = \text{constant} \quad \ldots \ldots \ldots \ldots \quad (1)$$

$$C = \frac{\gamma}{1-\gamma} I \frac{P_i}{P_c} \quad \ldots \ldots \ldots \ldots \quad (2)$$

$$-\frac{dC}{dI} = \frac{P_i}{P_c} \quad \ldots \ldots \ldots \ldots \quad (3)$$

Explanation

This extremely short model calls for little explanation. Equation (1) is the given circular transformation function. Equation (2) is the normal expenditure function. Equation (3) states that the technical exchange ratio or the opportunity cost of C in terms of I is equal to the economic exchange ratio or the price ratio. This equation may also be explained thus: in a state of equilibrium the marginal revenue from the production factors, in any use to which they may be put, must be equal, hence:

$$\frac{dC}{dL} \times P_c = -\frac{dI}{dL} \times P_i \quad \ldots \ldots \ldots \ldots \quad (3a)$$

In concrete terms, if a labour unit is withdrawn from I production (minus sign) the loss of revenue there is equal to the increase in revenue from the C production. The same applies to capital:

$$\frac{dC}{dK} \times P_c = -\frac{dI}{dK} \times P_i \quad \ldots \ldots \ldots \ldots \quad (3b)$$

From (3a) and (3b) we can readily deduce (3). With the aid of the
three equations of the model the three variables can be calculated, viz.
two volumes, C and I, and the price ratio.

Numerical Example

Let the constant be 2 and the propensity to spend on C be $\gamma = \frac{1}{2}$, then
the solution of the model is $C = 1$, $I = 1$, $\frac{P_i}{P_c} = 1$. This may be set out
graphically as in fig. 7.

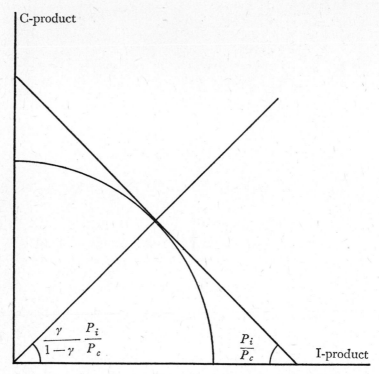

Figure 7. Equilibrium of demand and supply (closed economy)

OPEN ECONOMY

Free Trade

We shall now extend the foregoing model into an open economy.
We consider first the case of free trade in order to examine sub-

sequently the effect of import duties. Where equal techniques, resources and preferences exist, there is no reason for the existence of international trade. At least one of these data must differ in the countries involved. The way the mechanism works can be explained most simply by assuming identical techniques and resources in the two countries but different preferences.

Model 4.2   Free Trade

$$(X_c^1)^2 + (X_i^1)^2 = Z \quad\dotsfill \quad (1)$$

$$(X_c^2)^2 + (X_i^2)^2 = Z' \quad\dotsfill \quad (2)$$

$$S_c^1 = \frac{\gamma^1}{1-\gamma^1} \; S_i^1 \, \frac{P_i^1}{P_c^1} \quad\dotsfill \quad (3)$$

$$S_c^2 = \frac{\gamma^2}{1-\gamma^2} \; S_i^2 \, \frac{P_i^2}{P_c^2} \quad\dotsfill \quad (4)$$

$$-\frac{dX_c^1}{dX_i^1} = \frac{P_i^1}{P_c^1} = \frac{X_i^1}{X_c^1} \quad\dotsfill \quad (5)$$

$$-\frac{dX_c^2}{dX_i^2} = \frac{P_i^2}{P_c^2} = \frac{X_i^2}{X_c^2} \quad\dotsfill \quad (6)$$

$$S_c^1 + S_c^2 = X_c^1 + X_c^2 \quad\dotsfill \quad (7)$$

$$S_i^1 + S_i^2 = X_i^1 + X_i^2 \quad\dotsfill \quad (8)$$

$$S_c^1 P_c^1 + S_i^1 P_i^1 = X_c^1 P_c^1 + X_i^1 P_i^1 \quad\dotsfill \quad (9)$$

$$P_i^1 = P_i^2 \quad\dotsfill \quad (10)$$

$$P_c^1 = P_c^2 \quad\dotsfill \quad (11)$$

$$P_i^1 = 1 \quad\dotsfill \quad (12)$$

Explanation

The notation in this model is unfortunately more complicated than in the previous model because the real expenditure, denoted by S, is no longer equal in both countries to the production (X). The model gives for each country a production function (1) and (2), an ex-

penditure function (3) and (4), and a price function (5) and (6).
The third member of these equations is obtained by differentiation
of (1) and (2). Equations (7) and (8) represent real demand and
real supply as equal to one another, and in (9) the income and
expenditure of country 1 are represented as equal. This equation
implies equilibrium in the balance of payments of country 1 and
also, therefore, of country 2. Finally an exchange rate of 1 is
assumed in (10) and (11). Equation (12) is the nominal price
fixing basis.

Numerical Example

In our numerical example, where we are more concerned with finding
round figures than with realism, we assume that there is a marked
preference in country 1 for C products, so that $\dfrac{\gamma^1}{1-\gamma^1} = 3$ and in
country 2 $\dfrac{\gamma^2}{1-\gamma^2} = \tfrac{1}{3}$. The constant Z in equations (1) and (2) is
put at 2.

With these data we find the following solution for the twelve variables:

$$P_c^1 = 1 \qquad P_c^2 = 1 \qquad P_i^1 = 1 \qquad P_i^2 = 1$$

$$X_c^1 = 1 \qquad X_c^2 = 1 \qquad X_i^1 = 1 \qquad X_i^2 = 1$$

$$S_c^1 = \tfrac{1}{2} \qquad S_c^2 = 1\tfrac{1}{2} \qquad S_i^1 = 1\tfrac{1}{2} \qquad S_i^2 = \tfrac{1}{2}$$

$$F_c^1 = \tfrac{1}{2} \qquad M_c^2 = \tfrac{1}{2} \qquad M_i^1 = \tfrac{1}{2} \qquad F_i^2 = \tfrac{1}{2}$$

The last line gives the movement of trade, which is arrived at as follows:
country 1 consumes more I goods than it produces, and must therefore
import I goods: $S_i^1 - X_i^1 = M_i^1$; it consumes less C goods than it
produces, and can therefore export C goods: $X_c^1 - S_c^1 = F_c^1$. Similar
reasoning applies to country 1.

IMPORT DUTIES

The proportions in which I and C products are produced in a
country are determined, with a given transformation curve, by
the price ratio, since the production is not in equilibrium as long
as the real exchange ratio, i.e. the marginal substitution ratio of the
goods, differs from the price ratio. Graphically this means that the
production ratio is governed by the point at which the price curve
is tangent to the transformation curve.

If now country 2 imposes an import duty on the C product, the slope $\dfrac{P_i}{P_c}$ becomes smaller and the production point moves to the left along the supply curve, so that more C and less I will be produced. Suppose that the price of the I product remains unchanged; the home industry competing with the imports (the C industry) will then fetch a higher price, infra-marginal industries will be brought in and the production expanded. Although the price of the I product remains unchanged, the I industry will nevertheless be compelled to cut down on production, since the total production capacity remains the same, and therefore the expansion of C must be at the expense of I. The way the mechanism works may be interpreted as follows: owing to the expansion of C production, a demand will be made on production factors which will accordingly rise in price. The marginal I industries, assuming that the price of the I product remains constant, will see their costs exceed their revenue, and will consequently be forced to shut down. The indirect elasticity of the supply of I in relation to the price of C is thus negative *.

In the following we shall consider in a model the consequences of a protectionist policy. To be more concrete we may think of country 2 as Europe, which has a comparative advantage over the rest of the world (country 1) in the production of industrial goods (I goods) but which tries to protect its own agricultural produce (C goods) by imposing import duties.

PROTECTION UNDER INCOMPLETE SPECIALIZATION

Like the model used in the case of complete specialization, the model used here for incomplete specialization may be worked out in two phases. For the sake of brevity, however, we shall confine ourselves to the simultaneous model.

Model 4.3   Protection, Incomplete Specialization

$$X_c^1 x_c^1 + X_c^2 x_c^2 = S_c^1 s_c^1 + S_c^2 s_c^2 \quad \cdots \cdots \cdots \cdots \cdots \quad (1)$$

$$x_c^1 = {}_c\alpha_c^1 p_c^1 + {}_i\alpha_c^1 p_i^1 \quad \cdots \cdots \cdots \cdots \cdots \cdots \quad (2)$$

* For a more detailed treatment of the elasticities of supply, see appendix 2.

4

$$x_c^2 = {}_c\alpha_c^2\, p_c^2 + {}_i\alpha_c^2\, p_i^2 \quad\ldots\ldots\ldots\ldots\ldots\ldots \quad (3)$$

$$s_c^1 = {}_c\eta_c^1\, p_c^1 + {}_i\eta_c^1\, p_i^1 + \mu_c^1\,(q_{yc}^1\, p_c^1 + q_{vi}^1\, p_i^1 + q_{mi}^1\, t_i^1) \quad\ldots\quad (4)$$

$$s_c^2 = {}_c\eta_c^2\, p_c^2 + {}_i\eta_c^2\, p_i^2 + \mu_c^2\,(q_{yc}^2\, p_c^2 + q_{yi}^2\, p_i^2 + q_{mc}^2\, t_c^2) \quad\ldots\quad (5)$$

$$p_i^1 = p_i^2 + t_i^1 \quad\ldots\ldots\ldots\ldots\ldots\ldots\ldots \quad (6)$$

$$p_c^2 = p_c^1 + t_c^2 \quad\ldots\ldots\ldots\ldots\ldots\ldots\ldots \quad (7)$$

$$p_c^1 = 0 \quad\ldots\ldots\ldots\ldots\ldots\ldots\ldots \quad (8)$$

Explanation

The notation is the same as in the preceding models: capital letters denote absolute quantities, small letters relative deviations. The elasticities of demand (η), the elasticities of supply (α) and the elasticities of income (μ) are provided with a superscript, since they need not be the same in each country. The production shares q_{yc} and q_{yi} indicate the share of the value of the production of the C product or the I product in the value of the total *expenditure*:

$$q_{yc} = \frac{X_c\, P_c}{SP} \quad\text{and}\quad q_{yi} = \frac{X_i\, P_i}{SP},$$

where S denotes the total real expenditure and P its average price.

Equation (1) is the equilibrium equation, which equates the change in the real demand for the C product with the change in the real supply of that product. The absolute change is equal to the relative change times the initial value. Equations (2) and (3) give the relative or percentage changes in the supply as a function of the percentage price changes. The derivation of the elasticities of supply will be found in appendix 2. Equations (4) and (5) give the relative change in the demand as a function of prices and income.

As in model 3.1, we have assumed that the revenue from the import duty is income which is spent in the same way as the other income. The terms $q_{mc}^2\, t_c^2$ and $q_{mi}^1\, t_i^1$ express the changes in the revenue from the import duty as a percentage of the value of the expenditure *.

Income changes too, however, since the prices and production volumes in the domestic industries are altered. How large is this income effect? Put in another way, what is the magnitude of the percentage change in the value of the expenditure as a consequence of this change in income?

The situation is made a little complicated because the income from production (income at factor cost) need not be equal to the value of the

* See page 33.

expenditure (at market prices). This is particularly the case if an import duty is already imposed in the initial situation.

The relative change in total expenditure is equal to the weighted mean of the variations of income in the branches of industry, the weighting factors (q_y) being formed by the *share* of the income of each branch of industry in the *total expenditure*.

Expressed in a formula:

$$\frac{\Delta SP}{SP} = q_{yc} \frac{\Delta (CP_c)}{CP_c} + q_{yi} \frac{\Delta (IP_i)}{IP}.$$

Now the relative change in the value of production is approximately equal to the relative change in the volume plus the relative change in the price, assuming the price in the initial situation to be equal to unity.

The percentage increase in the value of the expenditure can thus be expressed in the formula:

(a) $$\frac{\Delta (SP)}{SP} = q_{yc} (x_c + p_c) + q_{yi} (x_i + p_i)$$

However, according to the theory of the elasticities of supply (appendix 2), we have:

(b) $$x_c = q_{xi} \, \delta \, p_c - q_{xi} \, \delta \, p_i$$

(c) $$x_i = - q_{xc} \, \delta \, p_c + q_{xc} \, \delta \, p_i$$

where q_{xc} and q_{xi} denote the *share* which the value of the C or I production represents in the value of the *total* production, and δ is the elasticity of substitution of supply. When it is a question of imposing an import duty starting from a situation of free trade, then q_x is equal to q_y. If, however, an import duty already exists in the starting situation, then $q_x = (1 + q_m t) \, q_y$. In both cases it is a matter of simple algebra to prove from (b) and (c) that the total change in production is

$$q_{yc} \, x_c + q_{yi} \, x_i = 0.$$

From (a) it now follows that the relative change in the value of expenditure is governed solely by the price changes according to the formula:

$$q_{yc} \, p_c + q_{yi} \, p_i.$$

The total effect on income is thus equal to the form between brackets in equation (4) of the model. Similar considerations apply to equation (5). Equations (6) and (7) give the relation between the prices, and the

last equation states that the price level of the C product remains unchanged. The change required in the terms of trade to create equilibrium
must therefore be achieved by changing the price of the I product.

Numerical Example

The data of the initial situation can be represented as follows in a
confrontation table of resources and expenditure:

INITIAL SITUATION

Country 1

Resources	Volume	Price	Value	Expenditure	Volume	Price	Value
X_c^1	10	$\times\ 1$	$=\ 10$	S_c^1	5	$\times\ 1$	$=\ 5$
X_i^1	10	$\times\ 1$	$=\ 10$	S_i^1	15	$\times\ 1$	$=\ 15$
			$\overline{20}$				$\overline{20}$
Imports				Exports			
M_i^1	5	$\times\ 1$	$=\ 5$	F_c^1	5	$\times\ 1$	$=\ 5$

Country 2

Resources	Volume	Price	Value	Expenditure	Volume	Price	Value
X_c^2	10	$\times\ 1$	$=\ 10$	S_c^2	15	$\times\ 1$	$=\ 15$
X_i^2	10	$\times\ 1$	$=\ 10$	S_i^2	5	$\times\ 1$	$=\ 5$
			$\overline{20}$				$\overline{20}$
Imports				Exports			
M_c^2	5	$\times\ 1$	$=\ 5$	F_i^2	5	$\times\ 1$	$=\ 5$

Further data *:

Direct elasticities of supply $\qquad$ $_c\alpha_c^1 = \,_c a_c^2 = \,_i\alpha_i^1 = \,_i\alpha_i^2 = +\tfrac{1}{2}$

Indirect elasticities of supply $\qquad$ $_i\alpha_c^1 = \,_i\alpha_c^2 = \,_c\alpha_i^1 = \,_c\alpha_i^2 = -\tfrac{1}{2}$

Direct elasticities of demand $\qquad$ $_c\eta_c^1 = \,_c\eta_c^2 = \,_i\eta_i^1 = \,_i\eta_i^2 = -1$

Indirect elasticities of demand $\qquad$ $_i\eta_c^1 = \,_i\eta_c^2 = \,_c\eta_i^1 = \,_c\eta_i^2 = \;\;0$

Income elasticities $\qquad$ $\mu_c^1 = \,\mu_c^2 = \,\mu_i^1 = \,\mu_i^2 = +1$

Country 2 imposes an import duty of 50 %, country 1 imposes no import duty, hence $t_c^2 = 0.5$; $t_i^1 = 0$.

If we insert these data into model 4.3 we can express all quantities in equation (1) as a function of p_i^2. Substitution of these quantities in (1) then gives a final equation with one unknown quantity, namely p_i^2. With the aid of the other equations we can then calculate all the variables. The variables x_i^1, x_i^2, s_i^1 and s_i^2 can also be calculated from the following alternative equations:

(2a) $\qquad x_i^1 = \,_c\alpha_i^1\, p_c^1 + \,_i\alpha_i^1\, p_i^1$

(3a) $\qquad x_i^2 = \,_c\alpha_i^2\, p_c^2 + \,_i\alpha_i^2\, p_i^2$

(4a) $\qquad s_i^1 = \,_c\eta_i^1\, p_c^1 + \,_i\eta_i^1\, p_i^1 + \mu_i^1\, (q_{yc}^1\, p_c^1 + q_{yi}^1\, p_i^1 + q_{mi}^1\, t_i^1)$

(5a) $\qquad s_i^2 = \,_c\eta_i^2\, p_c^2 + \,_i\eta_i^2\, p_i^2 + \mu_i^2\, (q_{yc}^2\, p_c^2 + q_{yi}^2\, p_i^2 + q_{mc}^2\, t_c^2)$

The results can be represented in a confrontation table of the changes in resources and expenditure.

CHANGES DUE TO IMPOSITION OF IMPORT DUTY

Country 1

Re-sources	Δ Volume	Δ Price	Δ Value	Expend-iture	Δ Volume	Δ Price	Δ Value
X_c^1	$10 \times -0.11 + 10 \times 0$		$=-1.1$	S_c^1	$5 \times \;\;0.11 +\;\; 5 \times 0$		$=\;\;0.5$
X_i^1	$10 \times \;\;0.11 + 10 \times 0.22$		$=\;\;3.3$	S_i^1	$15 \times -0.11 + 15 \times 0.22$		$=\;\;1.7$
			2.2				2.2
Imports				Exports			
M_i^1	$-2.7 + 5 \times 0.22$		$=-1.6$	F_c^1	$-1.6 +\;\; 5 \times 0$		$=-1.6$

---

* The elasticities of demand and supply were calculated on the basis of elasticities of substitution of demand and supply of 1 and income elasticities of 1. The relevant formulae are given in appendix 1 and 2. To avoid needless complications, we have disregarded second-order effects here.

Country 2

Re-sources	Δ Volume	Δ Price	Δ Value	Expend-iture	Δ Volume	Δ Price	Δ Value
X_c^2	10×0.14	$+\ 10 \times 0.5$	$= 6.4$	S_c^2	15×-0.015	$+\ 15 \times 0.50$	$= 7.3$
X_i^2	10×-0.14	$+\ 10 \times 0.22$	$= 0.8$	S_i^2	5×0.265	$+\ 5 \times 0.22$	$= 2.4$
T_c	20×0.25	$\times 0.50$	$= 2.5$				
			$\overline{9.7}$				$\overline{9.7}$
Imports				Exports			
M_c^2	-1.6	$+\ 5 \times 0$	$= -1.6$	F_i^2		$-2.7 + 5 \times 0.22$	$= -1.6$

The change in imports is calculated as follows. For country 1 the change in the value of the imports as a result of volume variations (briefly denoted as Δ volume) is: $(S_i^1 s_i^1 - X_i^1 x_i^1) = 15 \times (-0.11) - 10 \times 0.11 = -2.75$. The change in the value as a result of price variations (Δ price) is $(S_i^1 - X_i^1) p_i^2 = 5 \times 0.22 = 1.1$. The total change in the value of the imports is thus -1.6 (in round figures). Similarly, the change in the value of the exports is calculated as the difference between the variations in production and expenditure in respect of the exported product.

Simplified Model

The changes in imports and exports and in the terms of trade, resulting from tariff impositions, can also be calculated with the aid of a very simple model consisting of four equations.

Model 4.4　Import model

$$m_i^1 = \varepsilon_m^1 \left(p_i^2 + t_i^1 - p_c^1 \right) + \mu \left(q_{yi}^1 + q_{mi}^1 \right) t_i^1 \quad \ldots \ldots \ldots \quad (1)$$

$$m_c^2 = \varepsilon_m^2 \left(p_c^1 + t_c^2 - p_i^2 \right) + \mu \left(q_{yc}^2 + q_{mc}^2 \right) t_c^2 \quad \ldots \ldots \ldots \quad (2)$$

$$M_i^1 P_i^2 \left(m_i^1 + p_i^2 \right) = M_c^2 P_c^1 \left(m_c^2 + p_c^1 \right) \quad \ldots \ldots \ldots \quad (3)$$

$$p_c^1 = 0 \quad \ldots \ldots \ldots \ldots \ldots \ldots \quad (4)$$

Explanation

The above model is as difficult to grasp fully as it is easy to manipulate. Of course, one can say that ε_m^1 and ε_m^2 are import elasticities which indicate by what percentage the imports, in terms of demand, increase if the ratio of the price of the import product on the home market to the price of the home country's export product changes by one per cent. If we therefore assume, with Verdoorn * that the price of the export product does not change, then this import elasticity indicates the percentage by which imports change if the price of the import product on the home market changes by one per cent.

This elasticity, however, is an extremely abstruse notion, being the resultant of objective supply ratios and of subjective reaction coefficients like the elasticity of substitution of demand and supply and the income elasticity.

The complexity of the term 'import elasticity' appears from the formula which is derived in appendix 3:

$$\varepsilon_{mi}^1 = \frac{q_{yi} + q_m}{q_m}\left\{(1 - q_{yi} - q_m)\,\varphi - \mu.q_m\right\} + \frac{q_{yi}}{q_m}(1 - q_{xi})\,\delta.$$

Equally complicated is the term 'export elasticity', which indicates by what percentage exports, in terms of supply, increase if the export price level in relation to the price level of the home industry competing with imports increases by 1 %:

$$\varepsilon_{fc}^1 = \frac{1 - q_{yi} - q_m}{q_m}\left\{(q_{yi} + q_m)\,\varphi - \mu.q_m\right\} + \frac{1 - q_{yi}}{q_m}\,q_{xi}\,\delta.$$

The simplified model given here is in fact nothing but the reduced form of model 4.3. Equation (2) is deduced from (3) and (5) of model 4.3, and equation (1) from the alternative equations (2a) and (4a). If we substitute for the direct and indirect elasticities of demand and supply the corresponding formulae derived in appendix 1 and 2, we obtain, after some algebraic manipulation, the intricate coefficients which become no clearer if they are given the label of import elasticities. Equation (3) is a reduced form of the general equilibrium equations,

* P. J. Verdoorn, *Prae-advies voor de Vereniging voor de Staathuishoudkunde*, The Hague 1952, pp. 71—72.

which are incorporated in the income elasticity of unity and the equality of demand and supply reproduced in equation (1) of model 4.3.

Substitution of the data (page 52) in this model and in the elasticity formulae from appendix 3 leads by a shorter path to the same solution for p_i^2 as we found in the previous model. With this we can at once calculate the changes in imports and exports. To solve the other variables we must adopt the same procedure as in the previous model, that is via equations (2) to (7) and (2a) to (5a) of model 4.3.

RECIPROCAL DEMAND CURVES

The object of the above reasoning is that it gives the relation between the theory of general equilibrium and the theory of partial equilibrium, to which Marshall gave expression in his 'reciprocal demand curves' *.

For Marshall's G bales and E bales we can substitute our C product and I product. Under complete specialization these products represent, as in Marshall's case, a constant quantity of production factors. Under incomplete specialization this need not be so, and therefore our approach is somewhat more general. On the basis of a numerical example Marshall constructs two curves, one for each country, which are the loci of the volumes of imports and exports under existing conditions of supply and demand at various terms of trade. The point of intersection of these curves, one of which rises progressively and the other degressively, is the point of equilibrium, where the exports of the one country are equal to the imports of the other. From the form of the curves one can calculate the import and export elasticities.

We shall now proceed the other way around, and derive the reciprocal demand curve starting from the point of equilibrium, making use of the import and export elasticities which, as we have shown, are deduced from a general equilibrium analysis. In the point of equilibrium, at the applicable price ratio $\dfrac{P_c}{P_i}$ (given by the slope of the line that joins the point of equilibrium to the origin) demand and supply are in equilibrium with one another: $M_i^1 = F_i^2$ and $M_c^2 = F_c^1$. If now the price ratio increases by 1 %,

---

* A. Marshall, *The Pure Theory of Foreign Trade*, London 1930.

equilibrium for country 2 will be at a lower level, the import of C products decreases by ε_{mc}^2 % and the export of the I product by ε_{fi}^2 %. For the other country the equilibrium will be at a higher level, since the import of I and the export of C both increase. In this situation there is, it is true, equilibrium in the balance of payments, but supply and demand on the international market are not in equilibrium: the demand for the I product is greater than the supply, whilst the demand for the C product is smaller than the supply. By calculating the import and export elasticities for every new situation we can now construct a curve that will have roughly the same form as the familiar Marshallian curve.

Numerical Example

Let us suppose the following initial situation: Country 1 produces 200 C goods, of which it consumes 100 itself and exports 100 to country 2. This country produces 200 I goods, of which it consumes 100 itself and exports the remainder.

The price ratio on the international market is thus unity, and the import share for both countries is 0.5. Suppose now that the price ratio $\dfrac{P_c}{P_i}$ decreases by 10 % *, then the relative changes in imports and exports are

$$m_i^1 = \varepsilon_m^1 \, (p_c - p_i) = \left\{ (1 - q_m^1) \, \varphi + \mu \, q_m^1 \right\} (p_c - p_i) =$$
$$= 1.5 \times -0.10 \text{ (where } \varphi = 2, \, \mu = 1).$$
$$f_c^1 = \varepsilon_f^1 \, (p_c - p_i) = q_m^1 \, (\varphi - \mu) \, (p_c - p_i) = 0.5 \times -0.10$$

Likewise

$$m_c^2 = \varepsilon_m^2 \, (p_i - p_c) = 1.5 \times 0.10$$
$$f_i^2 = \varepsilon_f^2 \, (p_i - p_c) = 0.5 \times 0.10.$$

We then find the following pairs of numbers for the new situation:

$$M_i^1 = 85, \ F_c^1 = 95 \text{ and } M_c^2 = 115, \ F_i^2 = 105.$$

These points (disregarding second-order effects) lie on the price ratio line $\dfrac{P_c}{P_i} = 0.9$, whilst the balance of payments of each country remains

* To avoid the complications of second-order effects, one should really choose much smaller differences for constructing the curve.

in equilibrium, since the value of country 1's imports increases by, say, $(m_i^1 + p_i^1) = -0.15 + 0$ and the value of its exports by $(f_c^1 + p_c^1) = -0.05 - 0.10$.

Since the values of imports and exports were equal in the initial situation, they remain so in the new situation. The same holds for country 2.

For both points found we again calculate the import shares and related elasticities of imports and exports. These are again applied to a new price change, and so on. In this way we construct the reciprocal demand curve.

The advantage of this construction is that one can now clearly see that the reciprocal demand curve really conceals more than it discloses. The concepts of import and export elasticities, even in the simple case of complete specialization, are still far from clear. The relation between import and export elasticities, with which we are here concerned, is therefore particularly abstruse. The only insight which the curve can provide is that, where the price ratio is out of equilibrium, a gap occurs between supply and demand, but the cause of this gap—the interplay of substitutional and income effects under a given structure—is no longer comprehensible.

CONSEQUENCES FOR WELFARE AND FOR THE
DISTRIBUTION OF INCOME

The above confrontation table (pp. 53-54) of the changes in resources and expenditure shows something of the effects of a protectionist policy on national welfare.

Welfare in country 2 will increase. If we take as the welfare index the new volume of expenditure multiplied by the old prices, we see that it has risen by 1.1 or 5.5 %. The welfare in the rest of the world (country 1), however, shows a corresponding decline.

In regard to the distribution of income the following may be noted: if the C product (the agricultural produce) calls for the employment of a high proportion of labour, an expansion of C production in country 2 will make labour relatively scarcer and thus lead to an increase in the real wage and a drop in the return on capital. Conversely, in the rest of the world the distribution of income will change to the disadvantage of wage earners and to the advantage of capital owners.

Production Loss and Production Gain

In the previous chapter it was shown that prohibitive import duties reduce total production in that they hinder international specialization. Now it can be said that, in the case of curved transformation functions, every import duty is to some extent prohibitive, since it inhibits specialization at least partially. The drop in total production as a result of the imposition of import duties will be referred to as the production loss, and the rise in total production resulting from the abolition of import duties we shall call the production gain.

The production loss, and later the production gain, are not expressed in our models, the reason being that the elasticities of supply are such that the total production per country remains unchanged. Nevertheless, it is possible to find by approximation the order of magnitude of the production gain and of the production loss. We shall first consider the case where an import duty is imposed.

Fig. 8a shows a transformation curve with P as the production point in the initial situation. I is the export product and C the home product competing with imports. The slope of the price line CD gives the initial price ratio $\frac{P_i}{P_c}$. The price line itself is the locus of all combinations of C and I which have the same value at given prices. Since the initial prices are equal to one, this value is equal to the total volume of production. Now our elasticities of supply imply that the total volume of production before and after the imposition of the import duty remains unchanged; in other words, the value of the new production calculated at the old prices remains the same. In graphic terms this means that the new calculated production lies on the old price line. Let us say that this new point is point F.

The imposition of a duty on the import of C, however, causes a change in the domestic price ratio, and hence moves the production point along the supply curve. The *real* new production point A lies on the transformation curve and on the new price line DE, whose slope is equal to the new price ratio.

The real difference quotient $\frac{\Delta C}{\Delta I} = \frac{AB}{BP}$ is smaller than the original price ratio, but greater than the new price ratio. The actual difference quotient is approximately equal to the average of the old and the new price ratio. The point on the transformation curve that corresponds to this difference quotient lies on the transformation curve 'south-west' of the calculated point. This means that C increases less and I decreases more than was calculated. The difference between these points is the production loss.

Similar considerations apply to the abolition of the import duty (see fig. 8b). Here, too, the total volume of production remains constant in our model, but it must be remembered that the unit of volume for the home industry competing with imports is equal to the unit of value of the exporting country, the price of the competitive product in the importing country being $(1 + t)$, whilst this price in the exporting country is unity. The unit of volume is thus equal to the quantity of products that can be bought in the exporting country at a constant price of 1. The production point which we have calculated thus gives a combination of C and I having the same value as the original combination calculated at the new prices, which are both 1, disregarding the change in the terms of trade. The slope of this price line, however, is steeper than the actual difference quotient, whereas the slope of the old price line is less steep. As an approximation we can again say that the actual difference quotient is equal to the average of the old and new price ratio.

To calculate the production gain or the production loss we can now proceed as follows:

True value
$$-\tfrac{1}{2}\left(\frac{P_i}{P_c}^{\text{old}} + \frac{P_i}{P_c}^{\text{new}}\right) \Delta X_i = \Delta X_c$$

Calculated
$$-\Delta X_i = \Delta X_c$$

Effect on specialization
$$\left\{-\tfrac{1}{2}\left(\frac{P_i}{P_c}^{\text{old}} + \frac{P_i}{P_c}^{\text{new}}\right) + 1\right\}\Delta X_i =$$
$$= -\tfrac{1}{2}\left(\frac{P_i}{P_c}^{\text{old}} + \frac{P_i}{P_c}^{\text{new}} - 2\right)\Delta X_i.$$

Some examples will serve to make this clear. When a duty is imposed

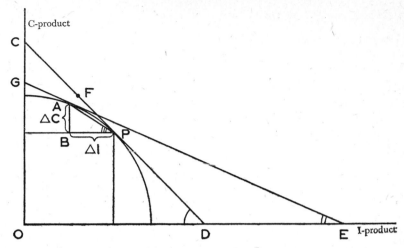

Figure 8a.   Secondary effects on supply curve
(Imposition of import duty)

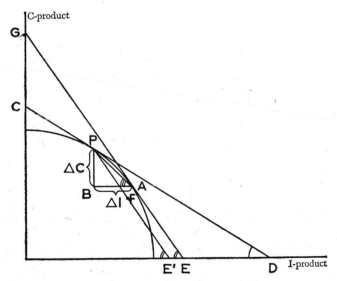

Figure 8b.   (Abolition of import duty)

on the import of C products, the price ratio $\dfrac{P_i\,\text{old}}{P_c} = 1$ and the price ratio $\dfrac{P_i\,\text{new}}{P_c} < 1$.

The true value of $\frac{1}{2}\left(\dfrac{P_i\,\text{old}}{P_c} + \dfrac{P_i\,\text{new}}{P_c}\right)$ i.e. the coefficient of ΔX_i, is then smaller in absolute value than 1, say 0.75. ΔX_i itself is negative, so that in reality the drop in I production will be compensated only up to 75 % by the increased C production. The volume of the total production thus decreases approximately * by 25 % of the calculated increase in the production of I.

When the import duty is abolished, the true value of the coefficient of ΔX_i will also be smaller in absolute value than 1. The change ΔX_i, however, is positive. Therefore the increase in I production will only partly be offset by the decrease in C production, and the result is a production gain.

The magnitude of the effect on specialization thus depends on the change in the price ratio, which is closely bound up with the level of the import duty and with the magnitude of the change in the volume of production of the export product; the latter in turn depends on the import duty, on the magnitude of the elasticity of substitution of supply and on the structure of the production in the initial situation.

Numerical Example

We can now calculate the production loss for the example given above (page 52 ff). Country 2 imposes an import duty on the C product. From the confrontation table on page 54 it appears that the increase in I production amounts to —1.4. The new price ratio is $\dfrac{1.22}{1.50}$. The production loss is therefore:

$$-\tfrac{1}{2}\left(\frac{1}{1} + \frac{1.22}{1.50} - 2\right) \times -1.4 = -0.13.$$

Country 1 does not impose an import duty, but its exports and its price ratio undergo a change. The C production decreases by 1.1 and the new price ratio between the C product and the I product is $\dfrac{1}{1.22}$.

---

* We say approximately because the calculated increase itself is, of course, not entirely exact, and moreover because the assumption that the true difference coefficient is equal to the average of the old and new price ratios is exact only where the transformation curve is a circle.

The production loss is therefore:

$$- \tfrac{1}{2}\left(\frac{1}{1} + \frac{1}{1.22}\right) - 2) \times - 1.1 = - 0.10.$$

The total production loss, caused by the abolition of the import duty, is thus 0.23 Even if an import duty of 50 % were imposed, we thus find a production loss which in all is no more than about one half per cent of the total production ($= 40$).

The effect on specialization may, however, be much greater if the elasticity of substitution of supply is high.

SUMMARY

The above considerations make it plain why the C producers in country 2, i.e. the farmers, will generally be in favour of a protectionist policy. It is also clear, however, that industry will not be particularly enthusiastic about agricultural protection behind high tariffs, because this forces them to restrict their production. From the national point of view there is an advantage to be gained from protection if the gain due to the improved terms of trade more than compensates for the loss in production.

Where one gains, however, another must lose. In this case the loser is the trade partner who must bear both the loss in his terms of trade and the production loss. The world as a whole suffers a setback.

Finally we should draw attention here to a difference between those models in which the elasticity of supply is zero and those in which it is positive. In the first case the change in imports will be less than in the second, because the higher price of the import product, as a result of the import duty, causes a drop in demand but the supply remains unchanged, whereas in the other case the imports decline not only because of the fall in demand but also because of the increased supply in the home industry competing with imports. It need not be surprising, therefore, that calculations concerning the effects of the abolition of import duties, which in fact presuppose complete specialization, i.e. imply a supply elasticity of zero in the competitive kome industry, result in only slight changes in imports.

CHAPTER V

VERDOORN'S APPROACH

The foregoing considerations on protection have revealed something of the effects that may follow from the imposition (and abolition) of import duties, both for the country that pursues an active policy in the matter of import duties and for the other countries which, passive in this respect, nevertheless feel the consequences.

In the following phase of our enquiry we shall consider what happens when several countries form a customs union, that is to say when the member countries of the union abolish import duties between themselves but maintain them entirely or in part in relation to non-member countries (henceforth called outsiders).

Before pursuing the lines of our argument and enquiring in our own way into the consequences of a customs union, we shall first consider how this problem has been approached by Prof. P. J. Verdoorn.

As early as 1952 this author published a brilliant treatise on European Integration*, a work that still belongs to the best that have been written on this problem. He was the first to attempt to solve the quantitative problem of the customs union in a system of simultaneous equations. I should like to preface any criticism I may make of his model by stating that the present book would never have been written without the stimulus of Verdoorn's original work.

UNDERLYING ASSUMPTIONS

The following are the main assumptions underlying Verdoorn's approach.

* P. J. Verdoorn, *Welke zijn de achtergronden en vooruitzichten van de economische integratie in Europa, en welke gevolgen zou deze integratie hebben met name voor de welvaart in Nederland?* (Background and prospects of economic integration in Europe, and the consequences of this integration on welfare in the Netherlands) Report presented to the Vereniging voor de Staathuishoudkunde, The Hague, 1952.

1. A customs union implies the removal of quantitative restrictions as well as the mutual abolition of import duties. Since, however, the effect of the removal of quantitative restrictions is difficult to measure, he confines himself in his model to the consequences of the changed tariff structure (page 77).

2. Full employment exists before and after the union is created, in other words the volume of total production remains constant. This means also that the imports of raw materials, disregarding the change in the structure of production, remain virtually unchanged (loc. cit.).

3. The members seek to maintain equilibrium in their balance of payments, i.e. in each country the changes in the value of imports must be equal to the changes in the value of exports. Moreover, Verdoorn assumes *in his model* that equilibrium exists in the balance of payments in the initial situation (page 118).

4. Should desequilibria occur in the balance of payments as a result of the modified tariff structure, these are corrected by adjusting the rate of exchange (loc. cit.).

5. The outsiders make no change in the value of their currencies: the correction of their exchange rate is zero. The other corrections are expressed in the outsiders' representative currency, the dollar (page 78).

6. Supply factors play no part in the model. It is assumed that supply immediately adjusts itself to demand, and that conversely, a change in supply has no effect on prices (page 77).

7. Domestic prices expressed in domestic currency remain unchanged (page 118).

8. The products are divided into nine categories. On the import market substitution takes place only between products of the same category. This assumption is not mentioned explicitly by Verdoorn, but follows from the definition of the concept 'elasticity of substitution of import demand' (page 72) and from the model employed (p. 118 ff.).

5

Notation and Definitions

To spare readers the labour of familiarizing themselves with Verdoorn's notation, we shall translate it where possible into the symbols hitherto used in this book.

Volumes

M^i volume of imports into country i

M^i_j volume of imports into country i from country j

M^i_{jH} volume of imports of product H from country j

Prices

P^i_{iH} export price of product H from country i in *dollars*

p^i_{iH} relative change of P^i_{iH}

P^i_{jH} market price of product H from country j in country i in the currency of country i $(i \neq j)$

p^i_{jH} relative change of P^i_{jH}

K_i, K_j exchange rates expressed in dollars

k_i, k_j relative change of K_i and K_j

t^i_{jH} change in the import duty on product H from country j in country i. The import duty is measured as the ad valorem percentage before the customs union is entered into.

Shares

q^i_{jH} share of the imports of product H from country j in the total imports of country i.

Elasticities

ε^i_H elasticity of imports, i.e. the percentage change in the imports of commodity H in country i when the import price of H changes by 1 % in relation to the domestic price level of H in country i.

β^i_{jH} elasticity of substitution of import demand, henceforth called share elasticity or Verdoorn elasticity, which indicates the percentage by which the share of commodity H from country j in the import market of country i rises when the ratio of the import price of H from country j increases by 1 % in relation to the import price level. The subscript j can be omitted, because the elasticity is the same for all countries.

$_se^i_{jH}$ the partial elasticity of demand or the partial elasticity of imports, which indicates by what percentage the imports of commodity H from country j on the import market of country i increase when the import price of commodity H from country s drops by 1 %. The direct partial elasticity of imports (s = j) is given by*:

$$_se^i_{jH} = \varepsilon^i_H \, q^i_{sH} + (1 - q^i_{sH}) \, \beta^i_H,$$

and the indirect partial elasticity of imports (s ≠ j) is given by:

$$_se^i_{jH} = \varepsilon^i_H \, q^i_{sH} - q^i_{sH} \, \beta^i_H,$$

where the q's represent the share of country s in the imports of commodity H into country i.

Simplification

There would not be much point in dealing in extenso with the operation of the full model specified by Verdoorn: he has done this himself better than we could do.

We shall therefore attempt rather to illustrate its operation by a greatly simplified example. We start with three countries: country 1 and country 2 enter into a customs union and apply an external tariff against the outsiders, country 3, amounting to the average tariff existing before the creation of the customs union. We further assume that there is only one product (differentiated per country) which enables us to omit the subscript H from all symbols.

All volumes are measured in constant dollars, so that in the initial situation all export prices are equal to unity.

The simplified model can now be represented as follows.

Model 5.1   Simplified Verdoorn Model

$$M^1_2 \, p^2_2 + \Delta M^1_2 + M^1_3 \, p^3_3 + \Delta M^1_3 = M^2_1 \, p^1_1 + \Delta M^2_1 + M^3_1$$
$$p^1_1 + \Delta M^3_1 \quad \ldots \ldots \ldots \ldots \ldots \ldots \quad (1)$$

$$M^2_1 \, p^1_1 + \Delta M^2_1 + M^2_3 \, p^3_3 + \Delta M^2_3 = M^1_2 \, p^2_2 + \Delta M^1_2 + M^3_2$$
$$p^2_2 + \Delta M^3_2 \quad \ldots \ldots \ldots \ldots \ldots \ldots \quad (2)$$

$$\Delta M^1_2 = M^1_2 \, (_2e^1_2 \, p^2_2 + _3e^1_2 \, p^1_3) \quad \ldots \ldots \ldots \ldots \quad (3)$$

---

* The derivation of these formulae was given in a subsequent report by P. J. Verdoorn, The intra-block trade of Benelux. Economic Consequences of the Size of Nations. *Proceedings of a Conference held by the International Economic Association.* Edited by E. A. G. Robinson. London 1960 pp. 291-329 Appendix A.

$$\Delta M_3^1 = M_3^1 \left({}_2e_3^1 \, p_2^1 + {}_3e_3^1 \, p_3^1 \right) \quad \ldots \ldots \ldots \ldots \quad (4)$$

$$\Delta M_1^2 = M_1^2 \left({}_1e_1^2 \, p_1^2 + {}_3e_1^2 \, p_3^2 \right) \quad \ldots \ldots \ldots \ldots \quad (5)$$

$$\Delta M_3^2 = M_3^2 \left({}_1e_3^2 \, p_1^2 + {}_3e_3^2 \, p_3^2 \right) \quad \ldots \ldots \ldots \ldots \quad (6)$$

$$\Delta M_1^3 = M_1^3 \left({}_1e_1^3 \, p_1^3 + {}_2e_1^3 \, p_2^3 \right) \quad \ldots \ldots \ldots \ldots \quad (7)$$

$$\Delta M_2^3 = M_2^3 \left({}_1e_2^3 \, p_1^3 + {}_2e_2^3 \, p_2^3 \right) \quad \ldots \ldots \ldots \ldots \quad (8)$$

$$p_1^1 \quad = k_1 \quad \ldots \ldots \ldots \ldots \ldots \ldots \ldots \quad (9)$$

$$p_2^2 \quad = k_2 \quad \ldots \ldots \ldots \ldots \ldots \ldots \ldots \quad (10)$$

$$p_3^3 \quad = k_3 \quad \ldots \ldots \ldots \ldots \ldots \ldots \ldots \quad (11)$$

$$p_2^1 \quad = k_2 - k_1 + t_2^1 \, . \ldots \ldots \ldots \ldots \ldots \quad (12)$$

$$p_3^1 \quad = k_3 - k_1 + t_3^1 \, . \ldots \ldots \ldots \ldots \ldots \quad (13)$$

$$p_1^2 \quad = k_1 - k_2 + t_1^2 \, . \ldots \ldots \ldots \ldots \ldots \quad (14)$$

$$p_3^2 \quad = k_3 - k_2 + t_3^2 \, . \ldots \ldots \ldots \ldots \ldots \quad (15)$$

$$p_1^3 \quad = k_1 - k_3 \, . \ldots \ldots \ldots \ldots \ldots \ldots \quad (16)$$

$$p_2^3 \quad = k_2 - k_3 \, . \ldots \ldots \ldots \ldots \ldots \ldots \quad (17)$$

$$k_3 \quad = 0 \quad \ldots \ldots \ldots \ldots \ldots \ldots \ldots \quad (18)$$

Explanation

The general form of this model resembles that of the reduced model in chapter IV.

Equation (1) states that the change in the value of country 1's imports is equal to the change in the value of its exports.

In the initial situation the value of the imports is $M_2^1 \, P_2^2 + M_3^1 \, P_3^3$. Disregarding secondary effects, we may write by way of approximation:

$$\Delta(M_2^1 \, P_2^2) = M_2^1 \Delta P_2^2 + P_2^2 \Delta M_2^1 \text{ and } \Delta(M_3^1 \, P_3^3) = M_3^1 \Delta P_3^3 + P_3^3 \Delta M_3^1.$$

The left-hand side is sufficiently explained if we remember that all prices in the initial situation are equal to unity and that therefore

$$\Delta P_2^2 = \frac{\Delta P_2^2}{P_2^2} = p_2^2 \text{ and } \Delta P_3^3 = \frac{\Delta P_3^3}{P_3^3} = p_3^3.$$

The right-hand side presents no difficulties either, if it is borne in mind that the volume of exports from country 1 to country 2 is the same as the volume of imports into country 2 from country 1.

Equation (2) is entirely analogous to equation (1). Equation (3) is a demand equation. The demand for the product imported from country 2 depends on the price changes on country 1's home market. These changes, expressed in percentages, are approximately equal to the price changes in national currency at the national frontier plus the change in the import duty. As is always the case with demand equations, the percentage change in demand (the form between brackets) is composed of the terms that denote the effect of the change in the price of the commodity in question (direct partial elasticity of demand times the relative change in the price of the commodity) and the effect of the change in the prices of other commodities (indirect partial elasticities of demand times the relative change in the other prices). This relative change of volume, multiplied by the volume in the initial situation, gives the absolute change in the volume of the demand for the product from country 2 on the import market of country 1. Equations (3) to (8) are built up in the same way.

Equations (9) to (11) state that the changes in the dollar prices of the exports are equal to the corrections of the exchange rate. If the domestic price of the exported product remains constant and the exchange rate of the dollar is increased by a certain percentage, then as the national currency becomes dearer in relation to the dollar, the domestic export price in dollars will also rise.

Equations (12) to (17) relate to the change of the price in domestic currency on the home market of the importing country. Just as exports become dearer in dollars when the exchange rate is increased, the imports by the same token become cheaper in home currency. The mutual changes in the exchange rates of two countries is thus the difference between these changes in relation to the dollar. Accordingly the price of an import product on the home market of the importing country will rise by the amount of the increase in the exchange rate of the exporting country minus the domestic increase in the exchange rate in relation to the dollar.

Furthermore the price on the home market changes in consequence of the change in the import duty.

Equation 18 is the expression of assumption 5.

Numerical Example

The structure of imports and exports and the value shares of imports are given:

$$M_2^1 = 10 \qquad M_3^1 = 10 \qquad q_{v2}^1 = 0.5 \qquad q_{v3}^1 = 0.5$$

$$M_1^2 = 10 \qquad M_3^2 = 10 \qquad q_{v1}^2 = 0.5 \qquad q_{v3}^2 = 0.5$$

$$M_1^3 = 10 \qquad M_2^3 = 10 \qquad q_{v1}^3 = 0.5 \qquad q_{v2}^3 = 0.5$$

The q's indicate the share of the imports from a particular country, denoted by the subscript, in the imports of the country denoted by the superscript. Since this concept differs from our own definition of import shares (which relates to the share of imports in the total expenditure in the importing country) we have added the subscript v.

Furthermore:

$$t_2^1 = - 0.2; \ t_1^2 = - 0.1; \ t_3^1 = - 0.05; \ t_3^2 = + 0.05.$$

The external tariff is thus fixed at the average import tariff of country 1 and country 2 in the initial situation.

The Partial Elasticities

The partial elasticities of imports can be calculated with the aid of Verdoorn's formulae. For example, if we follow Verdoorn and put the elasticity of imports at — 0.5 and the share elasticity at — 2, we have:

$$_2e_2^1 = q_{v2}^1 \ \varepsilon + (1 - q_{v2}^1) \ \beta = 0.5 \times (-0.5) + (1 - 0.5) \times$$
$$\times (- 2) = - 1.25$$

$$_3e_2^1 = q_{v3}^1 \ \varepsilon - q_{v3}^1 \ \beta = 0.5 \times (-0.5) - 0.5 \times (-2) = 0.75$$

The other elasticities can be found in the same way. In this special case all direct elasticities are — 1.25 and the indirect elasticities + 0.75.

Solution of the Model

Equations (12) to (18) and the calculated partial elasticities of demand are substituted in equations (3) to (8). After some manipulation we then find the following absolute changes in the import volumes:

$$\Delta M_2^1 = \quad 5 \ k_1 - 12.5 \ k_2 + 2.125$$

$$\Delta M_3^1 = \quad 5 \ k_1 + 7.5 \ k_2 - 0.875$$

$$\Delta M_1^2 = - \ 12.5 \ k_1 + 5 \quad k_2 + 1.625$$

$$\Delta M_3^2 = \quad 7.5 \ k_1 + 5 \quad k_2 - 1.375$$

$$\Delta M_1^3 = - \ 12.5 \ k_1 + 7.5 \ k_2$$

$$\Delta M_2^3 = \quad 7.5 \ k_1 - 12.5 \ k_2$$

Substitution of these changes and of equations (9) and (10) in (1) and (2) gives the two final equations with two unknown quantities:

$$15 \ k_1 - 7.5 \ k_2 - 0.375 = 0 \qquad k_1 = 0.117$$

$$-7.5 \ k_1 + 15 \quad k_2 - 1.875 = 0 \qquad k_2 = 0.183$$

We can now also calculate the percentage changes in the volume of imports:

$$\Delta M_2^1 = 0.42 \text{ or } 4\% \quad \Delta M_1^2 = 1.09 \text{ or } 11\% \quad \Delta M_1^3 = -0.08 \text{ or} - 1\%$$

$$\Delta M_3^1 = 1.08 \text{ or } 11\% \quad \Delta M_3^2 = 0.41 \text{ or } 4\% \quad \Delta M_2^3 = -1.42 \text{ or} - 14\%$$

The result is an extreme case but is a useful illustration. For although it was assumed that the average import duty for outsiders would remain equal to 15 %, the result of these changes in the exchange rate is that the price of the product imported from the outsider countries is in fact 12 % or 18 % cheaper, as a result of an appreciable improvement in the terms of trade.

The result of the customs union is that the advantage gained by the partner countries is at the expense of the outsiders, notwithstanding the fact that the average import duty on the outsiders' products is not changed. In other words, we have a marked example of passive discrimination.

ELASTICITY OF IMPORTS

In the two-country model (page 54) the concept 'elasticity of imports' has already been subjected to some criticism. We shall now consider this concept again with reference to a three-country model. The elasticity of imports may be derived most simply from the *fundamental* elasticities and the structure of demand, if we consider that in Verdoorn's *demand model* the partial elasticities of imports $_se^i_j$ are merely the direct and indirect elasticities of *demand* for the product imported from the various countries. If we equate Verdoorn's import elasticities with these elasticities of demand, we may write for a three-country model*:

$$_2e^1_2 = q^1_{v2}\, \varepsilon + (1 - q^1_{v2})\, \beta = {_2}\eta^1_2 = -\, q^1_{s2}\, \mu - (q^1_{s1} + q^1_{s3})\varphi \; . \qquad (1)$$

$$_3e^1_2 = q^1_{v3}\, \varepsilon - \qquad q^1_{v3}\; \beta = {_3}\eta^1_2 = -\, q^1_{s3}\, (\mu - \varphi). \; . \; . \; . \; . \qquad (2)$$

$$+ \quad \overline{}$$

$$\varepsilon \qquad\qquad = -\, (q^1_{s2} + q^1_{s3})\, \mu - q^1_{s1}\, \varphi \; . \; . \; . \qquad (3)$$

Since $q^1_{s2} + q^1_{s3} = q^1_m$ and further $q^1_m + q^1_{s1} = 1$, we can also write equation (3) as:

$$\varepsilon = -\, q^1_m\, \mu - (1 - q^1_m)\, \varphi \; . \; . \; . \; . \; . \; . \; . \; . \; . \; . \; . \qquad (3a)$$

The elasticity of imports is thus seen to consist of two components: the first component indicates the influence of the increase in real income when the average import price is lowered, the nominal income remaining constant. A 1 % reduction of the import price implies an increase of real income by q^1_m %. The second component indicates the extent to which the home product is supplanted by the imported product. Expressed as a percentage of imports, the supplanting of the home product will be greater the smaller is the share of imports in total expenditure. This, too, is reasonable, since an equal absolute supplanting of the home product as a percentage of imports will be greater the smaller is the share of imports.

It is evident from the above that the absolute magnitude of the elasticity of imports cannot be smaller than 1 if $\varphi \geqslant \mu$. Since the average elasticity of income fluctuates around the value 1, the elasticity of imports, given a share elasticity of -2, as Verdoorn assumes, (and which, as we shall prove, is equal to the elasticity of substitution of demand) must vary between —1.8 at an import share of 0.2 and —1.5 at an import share of 0.5. In any case, Verdoorn's

* The direct and indirect elasticities of demand are defined in appendix 1.

value of —0.5 for the elasticity of imports is not acceptable on theoretical grounds.

Further, Verdoorn's working hypothesis that the share elasticity (or the elasticity of substitution of demand, which we shall use) is equal to the average share elasticity for all countries and for all products, appears not to be consistent with the assumption that the elasticity of imports in all countries is equal to the average elasticity of imports. This is evident since, as we have demonstrated, the elasticity of imports is dependent on the structure of demand (in this case the import shares) which differs from one country to another.

Verdoorn's Elasticity and the Elasticity of Substitution of Demand

Verdoorn's elasticity indicates the 'percentage by which a particular country's share in the import market of another country increases when the ratio between the home price and the average import price level drops by one percent'.* The elasticity of substitution of demand as we define it, relates to the substitution not only of one import for another but also for the home product.

If now, as we assume, the elasticity of substitution for all goods is equal to the average elasticity, it can be shown that Verdoorn's elasticity is equal to the elasticity of substitution.

In the foregoing we stated that Verdoorn's partial elasticity of imports, for example $_3e_2^1$, is nothing but the indirect elasticity of demand $_3\eta_2^1$. We may write:

$$_3e_2^1 = q_{v3}^1 \, \varepsilon - q_{v3}^1 \, \beta \quad . \quad . \quad . \quad . \quad . \quad . \quad . \quad . \quad . \quad . \quad . \quad . \quad . \quad (1)$$

where β is the share elasticity. Further:

$$_3\eta_2^1 = - q_{s3}^1 \, \mu + q_{s3}^1 \, \varphi \, . \quad . \quad . \quad . \quad . \quad . \quad . \quad . \quad . \quad . \quad . \quad (2)$$

(see appendix 1).

Writing q_{v3}^1 as $\dfrac{q_{s3}^1}{q_m^1}$ and substituting for ε the formula found in the previous section, we can combine (1) and (2) in the following equation:

$$- q_{s3}^1 \, \mu + q_{s3}^1 \, \varphi = \frac{q_{s3}^1}{q_m^1} \times - (q_m^1 \, \mu + q_{s1}^1 \, \varphi) - \frac{q_{s3}^1}{q_m^1} \, \beta \, . \quad . \quad (3)$$

* Verdoorn report, page 72.

whence

$$- q_{s3}^1 \, \mu + q_{s3}^1 \, \varphi + q_{s3}^1 \, \mu + \frac{q_{s3}^1 \, q_{s1}^1}{q_m^1} \, \varphi = - \frac{q_{s3}^1}{q_m^1} \, \beta \quad \ldots \quad (3a)$$

or

$$\frac{q_{s3}^1 \, (q_m^1 + q_{s1}^1) \, \varphi}{q_m^1} = - \frac{q_{s3}^1}{q_m^1} \, \beta \quad \ldots \ldots \ldots \quad (3b)$$

Since the share of imports (q_m^1) plus the share of home demand (q_{s1}^1) is equal to unity by definition in as much as imports plus home demand constitute total expenditure) it is thus proved that the elasticity of substitution is equal to Verdoorn's elasticity, with the proviso that the elasticity of substitution is defined here as positive and Verdoorn's elasticity as negative.

Verdoorn's Assumption in regard to Substitution

It might be argued that, according to Verdoorn's assumptions, the elasticities of imports could nevertheless be smaller than unity, for Verdoorn assumes that there is no substitution betweeen the goods from different branches of industry (see assumption 8, page 65). The *average* elasticity of substitution could then be smaller than 1 and so also could be the elasticity of imports (see formula 3a, page 72).

This argument cannot hold water, however. If in fact no substitution takes place, we are still not entitled to conclude that the elasticity of substitution is zero.

Verdoorn's assumption that no *substitution takes place between the various types of goods* merely implies that the indirect elasticities of demand are zero, for in that case the demand for product B will not react on changes in the price of product A. The indirect elasticity of demand, however, will only be zero if the income elasticity is equal to the elasticity of substitution.* Since the value of the average income elasticity cannot be far from unity, Verdoorn's assumption thus implies an average elasticity of substitution of unity for goods from different branches of industry. For this reason it remains incorrect to assume an elasticity of imports having a lower absolute value than unity.

* See appendix 1.

The foregoing considerations are not merely theoretical, but have considerable practical significance. For example, a familiar argument from the theory concerning changes in exchange rates is that devaluation can only improve the balance of payments if the sum of the absolute values of the elasticities of imports and exports is greater than unity. Our considerations show, however, that this is always the case, since the absolute value of the elasticity of imports can never be lower than unity. Devaluation therefore always brings about an improvement in the balance of payments, in the longer run at least. (In the short run the elasticities are of course zero, in so far as there have not yet been any corrections.)

DISCUSSION OF VERDOORN'S MODEL

In view of the enormous complexity of an economic system, and the fact that so many factors are simultaneously operative in the creation of a customs union, it must be admitted that Verdoorn's model is relatively simple. Our complaint is really that it is too simple, and that it takes no account of factors essential to the operation of the mechanism.

Absence of Supply Factors

Verdoorn's model deals only with demand, and ignores the factors governing supply. He assumes that supply adjusts itself to demand, and that changes in supply have no effect on prices. He bases this assumption on the ground that the resultant changes in demand are in fact so slight that the supply can easily adjust itself to them *. This argument is not particularly convincing, for the new equilibrium is calculated by Verdoorn *on the assumption* that supply is not affected by price changes, whereas we have seen (page 43) that a model in which supply factors are operative leads to greater changes than a pure demand model. Verdoorn's assumption is a kind of 'self-fulfilling prophecy': *if* one discounts the supply factors, the changes will be negligible.

Now, in a later model ** Verdoorn did include the elasticity of supply, but it was the elasticity of supply *of exports*, a concept just as

* Verdoorn report, page 85.
** P. J. Verdoorn, The intra-block trade of Benelux, o.c. page 294.

complex as the elasticity of imports, and equally dependent on the structure of supply and demand.

Partial Model

Verdoorn's model is a partial-equilibrium model; it is confined to changes in imports and exports, but provides no guarantee that these changes will be consistent with changes in supply and demand on the home market.

We have already shown that his assumption of equal elasticity of imports for all countries and products is not tenable. Verdoorn makes the further assumption, with no attempt to substantiate it, that the expansion of one branch of industry will be compensated by the contraction of another, on the ground that the total production volume remains the same. But will supply and demand then be in equilibrium with one another?

Like the supply factors, the demand factors on the home market are also left by Verdoorn completely in the dark. The structure of demand and the existing elasticities on the home market are ignored. In particular, he also disregards the effects of tariff changes on income *, although these can also have a considerable influence on changes in imports and exports.

Moreover, is not the necessary adjustment of the structure of domestic production one of the most interesting and even burning questions of integration? In this respect, however, Verdoorn's approach adds little of value.

True, Verdoorn provides on page 90 of his report a table showing the shifts in the Dutch pattern of production as a result of the modified tariff structure, but this table is based on the assumption that domestic consumption remains unchanged in spite of the price changes on the home market. Verdoorn takes no account whatever of the extent to which home sales** are supplanted by imports, nor

* This is not the case as regards the effect of price changes on real income, since Verdoorn also includes these in his elasticity concepts.
** In a later version of the model: A customs' union for Western Europe — Advantages and Feasibility, *World Politics*, Vol. VI (1954) pp. 482-500, an elasticity of substitution of $\frac{1}{2}$ is assumed between home product and import product. This assumption implies that the indirect elasticities of demand are negative (see appendix 1), which seems an untenable proposition.

does he consider the mechanism which must bring supply into line with demand.

In the following chapters we shall attempt to produce a model which overcomes the objections to Verdoorn's model. Our model must therefore do justice to supply factors as well as demand factors; it must not be a partial but a total analysis; it must take account of substitutional and of income effects; finally it must satisfy the requirements of consistency: supply and demand must be in equilibrium in respect of volume as well as in respect of value.

CHAPTER VI

THE CUSTOMS UNION
UNDER COMPLETE SPECIALIZATION

Although a two-country model has enabled us to illustrate the consequences for all countries of the imposition or abolition of an import duty, the minimum number of partners in a customs union is three — the two countries entering into the union and the outsiders. In this chapter, and in the next, we shall therefore illustrate the problem of the customs union with some fictitious three-country models, in order to be able in the last chapter to provide a concrete illustration, with the aid of figures relating to the six countries of the European Economic Community.

COMPLETE SPECIALIZATION

In order to proceed from the more simple to the more complex, we shall begin with the case of complete specialization. By this we mean that each country makes its own product, of which it consumes one part itself and exports the remainder. The product exported from country 1 we shall refer to as product 1, and in the notation used the subscript will refer to the product and the superscript to the country. The same will apply to the products exported from country 2 and from country 3.

We assume provisionally that the balance of payments is in equilibrium in the initial situation, that is to say the expenditure is equal to the income. The expenditure equals the value of the consumption of the home product plus the market value of the import product. We assume that the prices of the export products in the country of origin and at the frontier of the importing country are equal to unity. The market price in the importing country is then $1 + t$, so that the market value of the import product is equal to the value of the imports plus the revenue from the import duty. Finally, the income is constituted by the value of domestic production and the revenue from the import duty. It is important to bear in mind the variation in the revenue from the import duty, since its removal, even though it is merely a nominal factor, has its effects on income.

Data

The data of the initial situation may be shown as follows in a confrontation table of resources and expenditure.

Country 1

Resources	Volume	Price		Value	Expenditure	Volume	Price		Value
X_1^1	100	$\times$ 1	=	100	S_1^1	80	$\times$ 1	=	80
T^1	20	$\times$ 0.2	=	4	S_2^1	10	$\times$ 1.2	=	12
					S_3^1	10	$\times$ 1.2	=	12
				104					104
M_2^1	10	$\times$ 1	=	10	F_1^1	20	$\times$ 1	=	20
M_3^1	10	$\times$ 1	=	10					
				20					20

Country 2

Resources	Volume	Price		Value	Expenditure	Volume	Price		Value
X_2^2	100	$\times$ 1	=	100	S_1^2	10	$\times$ 1.1	=	11
T^2	20	$\times$ 0.1	=	2	S_2^2	80	$\times$ 1	=	80
					S_3^2	10	$\times$ 1.1	=	11
				102					102
M_1^2	10	$\times$ 1	=	10	F_2^2	20	$\times$ 1	=	20
M_3^2	10	$\times$ 1	=	10					
				20					20

Country 3

Resources	Volume	Price	Value	Expend-iture	Volume	Price	Value
X^3_3	100	$\times 1$	$= 100$	S^3_1	10	$\times 1$	$= 10$
				S^3_2	10	$\times 1$	$= 10$
				S^3_3	80	$\times 1$	$= 80$
			100				100
M^3_1	10	$\times 1$	$= 10$	F^3_3	20	$\times 1$	$= 20$
M^3_2	10	$\times 1$	$= 10$				
			20				20

FIRST PHASE

We shall now consider what happens in the first instance if country 1 and country 2 abolish all import duties, between themselves and in relation to country 3. The latter country has no reason whatsoever to make any change in supply or demand, since the prices and its income are in the first instance unchanged. Nor is there any change in the volume of production in country 1 and in country 2, since we assume full employment both before and after the abolition of the import duty. Finally, there is no change either in the structure of production, because both countries remain completely specialized.

The changes that do occur are thus on the demand side. The abolition of the import duty entails two autonomous changes: the first is an autonomous change in prices and the second is a change in income resulting from the removal of the revenue from the import duty. How does demand react to these stimuli?

For the sake of convenience we shall consider the reaction in country 1. The reduction of income leads to a drop in demand for all products which, expressed in percentages, is the same for all products if, as we assume, the income elasticity is identical for all goods.

The prices of product 2 and of product 3, which amount to $1 + t^1$ in the initial situation, are reduced to 1 by the abolition of the import duty. The relative change is therefore $\dfrac{t^1}{1 + t^1}$. The demand for each of the three products will now react to this change of price in accordance with the existing elasticity of demand: the demand for product 2 will increase in accordance with the direct elasticity of demand, but this increase will be tempered by the negative influence of the reduction in the price of product 3. Similar considerations apply to product 3. The demand for product 1 will drop in accordance with the indirect elasticity of demand, in relation to the change in the price of product 2 and product 3. Since product 2 and product 3 are exclusively imported goods, the demand for the import of both goods will therefore increase. The part of product 1 which is not consumed by country 1 is exported, so that the supply of product 1 on the export market will increase by the same amount as domestic consumption decreases. The balance of payments remains in equilibrium because the reaction of the demand on all income effects is such that the effect of the drop in price on real income and the effect on nominal income of the abolition of the import duty are both absorbed by an equally large increase and decrease, respectively, of the demand. The reaction first referred to is bound up in the formulae for the elasticities of demand (see appendix 1) and the second is expressed in the term $\mu\, q_m{}^t$ (see page 33). The same procedure is adopted in respect of country 2.

The situation in this case, however, is not one of equilibrium. As we have seen, country 3 has no reason to make any change in its imports and exports, and moreover the changes in the imports and exports of country 1 and country 2 need not compensate one another. Price changes will therefore be necessary to create equilibrium in supply and demand. These changes will be discussed in the third phase.

Relation between the Change in Value and the Change in Volume
As shown in appendix 1, the direct and indirect elasticities of demand, as there deduced, are not exact quantities in so far as they relate to

6

volumes, since they ignore second-order effects, i.e. the products of relative changes. This is not so as regards the 'value elasticities', which indicate the relation between the relative change in the *value* of demand and the relative changes in prices. The change in volume can be more accurately determined by first calculating the change in value and by reducing this to the change in volume. In the case of the abolition of import duties this procedure is moreover very simple, because, as proved in appendix 1, the change in volume is then equal to the change in value minus the initial value times the tariff:

$$\Delta S = \Delta (SP) - SPt.$$

The absolute changes in the *value* of expenditure will henceforth be denoted by $\Delta \bar{S}$ and the relative changes in value by $\bar{s}$. Likewise, the 'value elasticities' will be denoted by $\bar{\eta}$.

The Model

The changes produced as a result of abolishing the import duty can now be calculated as follows.

Model 6.1. First Phase, Abolition of Import Duty

$$\Delta \bar{S}_1^1 = S_1^1 P_1^1 \left({}_1\bar{\eta}_1^1 \, p_1^1 + {}_2\bar{\eta}_1^1 \, p_2^1 + {}_3\bar{\eta}_1^1 \, p_3^1 - \mu \, q_m^1 \, t^1 \right). \quad . \quad (1)$$

$$\Delta \bar{S}_2^1 = S_2^1 P_2^1 \left({}_1\bar{\eta}_2^1 \, p_1^1 + {}_2\bar{\eta}_2^1 \, p_2^1 + {}_3\bar{\eta}_2^1 \, p_3^1 - \mu \, q_m^1 \, t^1 \right). \quad . \quad (2)$$

$$\Delta \bar{S}_3^1 = S_3^1 P_3^1 \left({}_1\bar{\eta}_3^1 \, p_1^1 + {}_2\bar{\eta}_3^1 \, p_2^1 + {}_3\bar{\eta}_3^1 \, p_3^1 - \mu \, q_m^1 \, t^1 \right). \quad . \quad (3)$$

$$\Delta S_1^1 = \Delta \bar{S}_1^1 - S_1^1 P_1^1 \, p_1^1 \; . \; . \; . \; . \; . \; . \; . \; . \; . \; . \; . \quad (4)$$

$$\Delta S_2^1 = \Delta \bar{S}_2^1 - S_2^1 P_2^1 \, p_2^1 \; . \; . \; . \; . \; . \; . \; . \; . \; . \; . \; . \quad (5)$$

$$\Delta S_3^1 = \Delta \bar{S}_3^1 - S_3^1 P_3^1 \, p_3^1 \; . \; . \; . \; . \; . \; . \; . \; . \; . \; . \; . \quad (6)$$

$$p_1^1 = 0 \; . \; . \; . \; . \; . \; . \; . \; . \; . \; . \; . \; . \; . \; . \; . \; . \; . \; . \quad (7)$$

$$p_2^1 = \frac{-t^1}{1 + t^1} \; . \; . \; . \; . \; . \; . \; . \; . \; . \; . \; . \; . \; . \; . \quad (8)$$

$$p_3^1 = \frac{-t^1}{1 + t^1} \; . \; . \; . \; . \; . \; . \; . \; . \; . \; . \; . \; . \; . \; . \quad (9)$$

The absolute change in value is equal to the initial value times the relative change thereof: $\Delta \bar{S} = SP\bar{s}$. The relative changes $\bar{s}$, however, are equal to the forms between brackets in equations (1) to (3).

Numerical Example

To keep the numerical example as simple as possible we shall equate the elasticity of substitution of demand φ with 1 and the income elasticity μ with 1. As will be seen from appendix 1, all direct and indirect *value* elasticities are then zero.

The tariff $t^1 = 0.20$, i.e. the reduction in the price of product 2 and product 3, amounts to $\dfrac{-0.20}{1.20} = -16.7\%$. The revenue from the import duty is 4 where the total expenditure is 104, hence $-q_m^1 \, t^1 = -3.84\%$. Substitution of these values in model 6.1 leads to the solution:

$$\Delta \bar{S}_1^1 = -3.07 \qquad\qquad \Delta S_1^1 = -3.07$$

$$\Delta \bar{S}_2^1 = -0.46 \qquad\qquad \Delta S_2^1 = 1.54$$

$$\Delta \bar{S}_3^1 = -0.46 \qquad\qquad \Delta S_3^1 = 1.54$$

We now arrive at the new confrontation table of resources and expenditure after the first phase.

FIRST PHASE, ABOLITION OF IMPORT DUTIES

Country 1

Resources	Volume	Price	Value	Expenditure	Volume	Price	Value
X_1^1	100	$\times 1$	$= 100$	S_1^1	76.92	$\times 1 =$	76.92
T^1			0	S_2^1	11.54	$\times 1 =$	11.54
				S_3^1	11.54	$\times 1 =$	11.54
			100				100
M_2^1	11.54	$\times 1 =$	11.54	F_1^1	23.08	$\times 1 =$	23.08
M_3^1	11.54	$\times 1 =$	11.54				
			23.08				23.08

The changes in imports and exports, in which we are primarily interested, are thus:

$$\Delta M_2^1 = 1.54; \qquad \Delta M_3^1 = 1.54; \qquad \Delta F_1^1 = 3.08.$$

Along the same lines we can also calculate the changes in the imports of country 2 if it abolishes its duty of 10 %:

$$\Delta M_1^2 = 0.78; \qquad \Delta M_3^2 = 0.78; \qquad \Delta F_2^2 = 1.56.$$

In this way we have thus found the primary consequences of a general abolition of import duties. In the case of a customs union, however, the partner countries impose a common external tariff against the outsiders. Let us assume that this tariff is 15 %. The consequences of this will be calculated in the second phase.

SECOND PHASE

In order to calculate the consequences of the external tariff at 15 %, we shall take the original volumes as our starting point. It might otherwise be objected that our analysis is not in accordance with reality, for one does not first abolish all import duties, and then impose an external tariff immediately afterwards. The external tariff is brought to its new level at the same time as the internal tariff is abolished. For this reason we start from the original volumes.

It should be remarked, perhaps unnecessarily, that the breakdown into three phases does not relate to consecutive phases in terms of time, but is merely an instrument of analysis. The result of the calculations by one method or the other differs so little, however, that the advantage in analysis gained in this way amply compensates for its lower accuracy.

At the risk of straying into over-refinements and making the whole exposition unclear, we shall nevertheless give an *exact* treatment of the second phase of this model. In the later models (chapters 7 and 8), which become increasingly comprehensive and thus inevitably more complicated, the second phase will be calculated, for the sake of simplicity, without taking second-order effects into account.

As proved in appendix 1, the change in the volume of product 1 and of product 2 in the second phase is equal to the change in value, since no import duties are imposed on these products. The change in the volume of product 3 is:

$$\Delta S_3^1 = \frac{1}{1 + p_3^1} (\bar{S}_3^1 \bar{s}_3^1 - S_3^1 p_3^1)$$

since the external tariff is specially imposed on imports from country 3.

This brings us to the model for the second phase.

Model 6.2   Second Phase. Imposition of External Tariff

$$\Delta S_1^1 = \bar{S}_1^1 (_3\bar{\eta}_1^1 p_3^1 + \mu y^1) \cdot \cdot \cdot \cdot \cdot \cdot \cdot \cdot \cdot \cdot \cdot \cdot \cdot \quad (1)$$

$$\Delta S_2^1 = \bar{S}_2^1 (_3\bar{\eta}_2^1 p_3^1 + \mu y^1) \cdot \cdot \cdot \cdot \cdot \cdot \cdot \cdot \cdot \cdot \cdot \quad (2)$$

$$\Delta S_3^1 = \frac{1}{1 + p_3^1} \{\bar{S}_3^1 (_3\bar{\eta}_3^1 p_3^1 + \mu y^1) - S_3^1 p_3^1\} \cdot \cdot \cdot \cdot \quad (3)$$

$$y^1 = \frac{(S_3^1 + \Delta S_3^1) t_3^1}{Y^1} \cdot \cdot \cdot \cdot \cdot \cdot \cdot \cdot \cdot \cdot \cdot \cdot \cdot \quad (4)$$

$$p_3^1 = t_3^1 \cdot \cdot \cdot \cdot \cdot \cdot \cdot \cdot \cdot \cdot \cdot \cdot \cdot \cdot \cdot \cdot \cdot \cdot \quad (5)$$

As there is no change in the prices of product 1 and product 2, the terms pertaining to these have been omitted.

Numerical Example

To solve the model we substitute (4) and (5) in (3). Since $_3\bar{\eta}_3^1 = 0$, the relevant term may be omitted.

(a) $$\Delta S_3^1 = \frac{1}{1 + t_3^1} \left\{ \bar{S}_3^1 \mu \frac{(S_3^1 + \Delta S_3^1) t_3^1}{Y} - S_3^1 t_3^1 \right\}$$

or

(b) $$\left(1 - \frac{\bar{S}_3^1 \mu t_3^1}{(1 + t_3^1) Y^1}\right) \Delta S_3^1 = \frac{\bar{S}_3^1 \mu S_3^1 t_3^1}{(1 + t_3^1) Y^1} - \frac{S_3^1 t_3^1}{1 + t_3^1}$$

Inserting the known values, we obtain:

(c) $$\left(1 - \frac{1.5}{115}\right) \Delta S_3^1 = \frac{0.15 - 1.5}{1.15}$$

(d) $$\Delta S_3^1 = -1.19$$

Next we calculate the relative change in income:

(e) $\quad y^1 = \dfrac{0.15\,(10 - 1.19)}{100} = 0.013$

Since the indirect elasticities in this case are zero, the changes ΔS_1^1 and ΔS_2^1 can at once be determined.

The second phase thus leads to the following confrontation table of resources and expenditure for country 1.

SECOND PHASE. IMPOSITION OF EXTERNAL TARIFF

Country 1

Resources	Volume	Price	Value	Expenditure	Volume	Price	Value
X_1^1	100	$\times\ 1$	$= 100.00$	S_1^1	81.06	$\times\ 1$	$= 81.06$
T_3^1	8.81	$\times\ 0.15 =$	1.32	S_2^1	10.13	$\times\ 1$	$= 10.13$
				S_3^1	8.81	$\times\ 1.15$	$= 10.13$
			101.32				101.32
M_2^1	10.13	$\times\ 1$	$= 10.13$	F_1^1	18.94	$\times\ 1$	$= 18.94$
M_3^1	8.81	$\times\ 1$	$= 8.81$				
			18.94				18.94

The changes for country 2 are *mutatis mutandis* the same as for country 1

$$\Delta S_1^2 = 0.13; \qquad \Delta S_2^2 = 1.06; \qquad \Delta S_3^2 = -1.19$$

THIRD PHASE

Restoration of Equilibrium

The situation which arises after the second phase is not one of equilibrium, for supply and demand are no longer balanced. The supply of the three products remains unchanged, but the demand does not. To calculate the resultant gap between supply and demand, we must add together the changes that have occurred in the two phases and in the two countries.

In order to correct this disequilibrium, the prices will have to undergo relative changes. The price of a product for which there is a deficit demand after the two phases will have to be relatively lower, whereas the price of a product for which there is a surplus demand will have to be relatively higher. Since we are concerned with *price ratios*, we can also keep one price constant and let the other two vary.

We have already mentioned (page 35) that our model implies equilibrium in the balance of payments, in view of the fact that the income elasticity is equal to unity. It has also been shown that, where supply and demand in respect of one product are balanced in a two-country model, the same must apply to the other product. With a three-country model it can be proved in the same way that, given equilibrium in the case of two products, supply and demand in respect of the third product will also balance.

We shall assume that the price of the third product remains unchanged, and that the price levels of country 1 and country 2 are properly adjusted.

The Model

To prevent the model becoming non-linear and thus completely unwieldy, which it would certainly be if extended to six countries, we shall disregard second-order effects in our model of the third phase. We shall thus use the 'volume elasticities' as arrived at in appendix 1.

Model 6.3   Third Phase. Change in the Terms of Trade

$$\Delta S_1 + S_1^1 s_1^1 + S_1^2 s_1^2 + S_1^3 s_1^3 = 0 \quad \ldots \ldots \ldots \quad (1)$$

$$\Delta S_2 + S_2^1 s_2^1 + S_2^2 s_2^2 + S_2^3 s_2^3 = 0 \quad \ldots \ldots \ldots \quad (2)$$

$$s_1^1 = {}_1\eta_1^1 p_1 + {}_2\eta_1^1 p_2 + \mu p_1 \cdot \quad \ldots \ldots \ldots \quad (3)$$

$$s_1^2 = {}_1\eta_1^2 p_1 + {}_2\eta_1^2 p_2 + \mu p_2 \cdot \quad \ldots \ldots \ldots \quad (4)$$

$$s_1^3 = {}_1\eta_1^3 p_1 + {}_2\eta_1^3 p_2 \quad \ldots \ldots \ldots \quad (5)$$

$$s_2^1 = {}_1\eta_2^1\, p_1 + {}_2\eta_2^1\, p_2 + \mu\, p_1 \quad \ldots \ldots \ldots \ldots \quad (6)$$

$$s_2^2 = {}_1\eta_2^2\, p_1 + {}_2\eta_2^2\, p_2 + \mu\, p_2 \quad \ldots \ldots \ldots \ldots \quad (7)$$

$$s_2^3 = {}_1\eta_2^3\, p_1 + {}_2\eta_2^3\, p_2 \quad \ldots \ldots \ldots \ldots \ldots \quad (8)$$

Explanation

Since there is no change in production, the sum of the changes in real expenditure per product must be zero. The deficit in demand $\Delta\, S_1$, which is the primary effect resulting from the abolition of import duties and the imposition of an external tariff, must be compensated by a rise in demand brought about by price changes. The necessary change in the demand for product 1 in the various countries (the second, third and fourth terms of the first equation) can indeed be written as a function of the relative price changes if we substitute equations (3) to (5) in (1).

Apart from the terms that indicate the reaction to the price changes, equations (3) and (4) contain a term which represents the effect of the price changes on income: for if the price of product 1 falls by a certain percentage, the income from the production must also fall by the same percentage.

The model is solved quite simply by filling-in the values found for $\Delta\, S_1$ and $\Delta\, S_2$, and by substituting equations (4) to (8) in (1) and (2). Using the prices found we then calculate the relative and absolute changes in demand.

Finally, using the same prices, we can calculate the relative and absolute changes in the demand for product 3 from the following three equations:

$$s_3^1 = {}_1\eta_3^1\, p_1 + {}_2\eta_3^1\, p_2 + \mu\, p_1 \quad \ldots \ldots \ldots \ldots \quad (9)$$

$$s_3^2 = {}_1\eta_3^2\, p_1 + {}_2\eta_3^2\, p_2 + \mu\, p_2 \quad \ldots \ldots \ldots \quad (10)$$

$$s_3^3 = {}_1\eta_3^3\, p_1 + {}_2\eta_3^3\, p_2 \quad \ldots \ldots \ldots \ldots \quad (11)$$

Numerical Example

By substituting in equations (1) and (2) the changes $\Delta\, S_1$ and $\Delta\, S_2$ and equations (3) to (8), we arrive at the following two expressions in which the price changes sought are the two unknown quantities:

$$20\, p_1 - 10\, p_2 = -1.10 \qquad\qquad p_1 = -0.034$$

$$-10\, p_1 + 20\, p_2 = +1.172 \qquad\qquad p_2 = 0.041$$

The changes in expenditure are now calculated by inserting the prices found in equations (3) to (11), and then multiplying the resultant relative changes by the volumes of expenditure in the initial situation.

$\Delta S_1^1 = \quad 0$ $\Delta S_1^2 = 0.76$ $\Delta S_1^3 = \quad 0.34$

$\Delta S_2^1 = -0.76$ $\Delta S_2^2 = 0$ $\Delta S_2^3 = -0.41$

$\Delta S_3^1 = -0.35$ $\Delta S_3^2 = 0.41$ $\Delta S_3^3 = \quad 0$

Our system of equations brings forth not only the rabbits we put into the hat, i.e. the corrections of the disequilibria in supply and demand, but also the instruments to catch our rabbits, namely the price changes necessary to restore the balance.

We can now gather-in the harvest of all changes brought about by the customs union. The final result is found by adding together the changes in the three phases. We shall represent this result for country 1 in a confrontation table of the changes in resources and expenditure, divided over the three phases. For the other countries we shall indicate only the changes in imports and exports. The interested reader has all the data he requires for drawing up complete confrontation tables for the other countries too.

The final confrontation of the changes in resources and expenditure for country 1, and the changes in imports and exports in country 2 and 3, will be found on page 90.

RELATION BETWEEN PRICE CHANGES AND RATE OF EXCHANGE

We have chosen in our model an adjustment of the export price level as the instrument designed to restore equilibrium. It might be asked what the relation is between a price change and a possible alteration of the exchange rate. In the present case the relation is particularly straightforward, since the percentage devaluation or appreciation with respect to the outsiders' unit of currency is equal to the fall or rise in price of the exported product. As the total volume of production remains unchanged, the remuneration of the production factors must increase or decrease by the same percentage as the value of the production at factor cost. Now, it makes no difference whether we let all prices in

COMPLETE SPECIALIZATION

Country 1

Resources	Δ Volume	Δ Price	Δ Value	Expend-iture	Δ Volume	Δ Price	Δ Value
X_1^1	0	+ 0		S_1^1	−3.07	+ 0	
	0	+ 0			1.06	+ 0	
	0	− 3.43			0	− 2.74	
	0	− 3.43 =	− 3.43		−2.01	− 2.74 =	− 4.75
T^1			− 4.00	S_2^1	1.54	− 2.00	
					0.13	− 0	
					−0.76	+ 0.41	
					0.91	− 1.59 =	− 0.68
T_3^1			1.32	S_3^1	1.54	− 2.00	
					−1.19	+ 1.32	
					−0.35	+ 0	
					−0.00	− 0.68 =	− 0.68
			− 6.11				− 6.11
M_2^1	0.91	+ 0.41 =	1.32	F_1^1	2.01	− 0.69 =	1.32
M_3^1	0.00	+ 0.00 =	0.00				
			1.32				1.32

CHANGES IN IMPORTS AND EXPORTS

Country 2

Imports	Δ Volume	Δ Price	Δ Value	Exports	Δ Volume	Δ Price	Δ Value
M_1^2	1.67	− 0.34 =	1.33	F_2^2	0.50	+ 0.83 =	1.33
M_3^2	0.00	+ 0	= 0.00				
			1.33				1.33

Country 3

Imports	Δ Volume	Δ Price	Δ Value	Exports	Δ Volume	Δ Price	Δ Value
M_1^3	0.34 —	0.34	= 0	F_3^3	0 +	0	= 0
M_2^3	—0.41 +	0.41	= 0				
			0				0

national currency rise by a certain percentage, with the outsiders' prices remaining constant, or whether we keep our own price level constant and appreciate the value of our own currency. As far as the price ratios on the home market are concerned, it therefore makes no difference whether the equilibrium is created by appreciating the domestic currency or by raising the export price level. The results of the latter method can be reduced to the former by lowering all prices on the home market by the percentage of appreciation.

CHANGE IN WELFARE

A model based on complete specialization is obviously not suitable for demonstrating the effect of the customs union on specialization. Where complete specialization prevails, it is not possible to specialize still further. However, the fact that the total production, and hence the total welfare, remains the same, does not imply that there will be no effects on welfare in the individual countries. The customs union evidently has an influence on the *distribution* of the product.

The simplest method of calculating the effect on real income is to divide the nominal income by the average price level. If now, given unchanged production, the nominal income and the nominal expenditure increase or decrease by an equal amount, then welfare will increase if the average price level of the real expenditure rises less or falls more than the average price level of the production. Where both change by the same percentage, we have an inflationary or deflationary phenomenon which leaves the total real income unaffected. The changes in the revenue from the import duty can be disregarded in this case, because they are just as great on the production side as on the expenditure side.

Applied to our numerical example, and ignoring second-order effects, this means that in country 1 the price level on the production side falls by 3.4 %. On the expenditure side the price level drops by 2.3 %, so that we must conclude that real income in country 1 falls by 1.1 %. In the same way we find that real income in country 2 will rise by 1.2 %, and fall in country 3 by 0.1 %. One country gains by the other's loss.

The same result is arrived at if we multiply the improvement or deterioration of the terms of trade by the relevant import share. Thus, the terms of trade of country 1 deteriorate in relation to those of country 2 both because its own export price is lowered and because the price of imports from that country is increased on balance by 7.6 %. This, multiplied by the import share q_{m2}^1, yields a drop in real income of 0.76 %. In relation to country 3 the terms of trade decline by 3.4 %, so that the effect on real income is 0.34 %. The result of this calculation is thus identical with that of the previous one.

The conclusion we may draw from the foregoing as to the effect of the customs union on welfare is that the partners of the union have jointly improved their welfare at the expense of the outsiders, but that the partner country that was least protectionist in the initial stage is the one that reaps the profit, so much so in fact that the country that had originally imposed the highest import duties is ultimately worse off.

The Outsiders

In the numerical example considered here the outsiders have in effect no advantage or disadvantage in the customs union. This need not be so, however, but is a consequence of the perfect symmetry of the example and of the chosen tariffs and elasticities. The extent to which the outsiders will gain or lose by the customs union depends primarily on the level of the common external tariff. This may be illustrated as follows.

The changes in the terms of trade of the union countries in relation to the outsiders may be written as a function of the external tariff t_3. If we disregard the secondary effects of the changes in volume, this function is even a linear one. In the final equations on page 88 the constants are calculated as the sum of the changes in the volumes from the first and second phases. In the first phase the

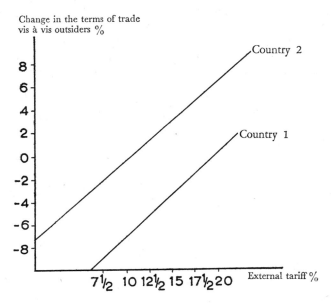

Change in the terms of trade vis à vis outsiders %

Country 2

Country 1

7½ 10 12½ 15 17½20   External tariff %

Figure 9. Relation between the level of the external tariff and the change in the terms of trade vis à vis outsiders

external tariff is irrelevant, but the changes in the second phase are a function of the external tariff. If we represent the changes in the first phase as $\Delta^* S_1$ and $\Delta^* S_2$, respectively, we can write the following equations:

$$- 20p_1 + 10p_2 = \Delta^* S_1 + (S_1^1 q_{m3}^1 + S_1^2 q_{m3}^2) t_3 \quad \cdot \quad \cdot \quad (1)$$

$$- 10p_1 + 20p_2 = \Delta^* S_2 + (S_2^1 q_{m3}^1 + S_2^2 q_{m3}^2) t_3 \quad \cdot \quad \cdot \quad (2)$$

After solving the set of equations for two values of t_3, we can find by extrapolation in a graph the changes in the terms of trade pertaining to any value of the external tariff *. See fig. 9.

This brings us to the important conclusion that the average change in the terms of trade in relation to the outsiders can always be reduced to zero by manipulating the external tariff: the outsiders need not therefore suffer any disadvantage from the union. On the other hand, an unduly low external tariff may adversely affect the terms of trade of the union as a whole.

* This method is due to P. J. Verdoorn, Prae-advies, page 87.

CHAPTER VII

THE CUSTOMS UNION
UNDER INCOMPLETE SPECIALIZATION

The case of complete specialization is not the most probable if it is assumed that the cost curve per branch of industry shows a rising trend, or, as we put it in a past chapter (page 44) if the transformation line is curved. In this chapter we shall therefore assume that specialization is not complete and that each of the three countries involved in the union produces all three products itself, but that only one product, which we shall call the export product, is both consumed and exported in each case, whilst the two other products are also imported.

Let us consider for a moment the initial situation in country 1. It produces product 1, one part of which it consumes itself and exports the remainder. The price of this product is unity. It also produces and imports product 2 and product 3, on which an ad valorem import duty is imposed amounting to t^1. The price of this imported product on the home market is therefore $(1 + t^1)$ if the import price is again put at unity. In the initial situation, country 1 has so expanded its production of commodities 2 and 3 that the relevant price is also $(1 + t^1)$. A similar situation exists in country 2 and country 3.

We shall start from the data, given on pp. 96—97.

Comparative Costs

The three countries are seen to have a clear advantage in comparative costs as far as the export product is concerned. In terms of product 2 and 3, product 1 is cheaper in country 1 than in country 2 or 3. The same applies mutatis mutandis to the other countries. The cost differences are artificially maintained by the import duties. If these did not exist, the exchange mechanism would ensure that the production of the export product would be so much expanded in the exporting country, and the production of the same

Country 1

Resources	Volume	Price	Value	Expenditure	Volume	Price	Value
X_1^1	80	× 1 =	80	S_1^1	60	× 1 =	60
X_2^1	10	× 1.2 =	12	S_2^1	20	× 1.2 =	24
X_3^1	10	× 1.2 =	12	S_3^1	20	× 1.2 =	24
T^1			4				
			108				108
M_2^1	10	× 1 =	10	F_1^1	20	× 1 =	20
M_3^1	10	× 1 =	10				
			20				20

Country 2

Resources	Volume	Price	Value	Expenditure	Volume	Price	Value
X_1^2	10	× 1.1 =	11	S_1^2	20	× 1.1 =	22
X_2^2	80	× 1 =	80	S_2^2	60	× 1 =	60
X_3^2	10	× 1.1 =	11	S_3^2	20	× 1.1 =	22
T^2			2				
			104				104
M_1^2	10	× 1 =	10	F_2^2	20	× 1 =	20
M_3^2	10	× 1 =	10				
			20				20

Country 3

Resources	Volume	Price		Value	Expend-iture	Volume	Price		Value
X_1^3	10	× 1	=	10	S_1^3	20	× 1	=	20
X_2^3	10	× 1	=	10	S_2^3	20	× 1	=	20
X_3^3	80	× 1	=	80	S_3^3	60	× 1	=	60
				100					100
M_1^3	10	× 1	=	10	F_3^3	20	× 1	=	20
M_2^3	10	× 1	=	10					
				20					20

commodity so far reduced in the importing country, as ultimately to equalize the prices at a given rate of exchange. The abolition of the import duty will therefore make this levelling mechanism operative. (See the Scitovsky figure on page 108.)

Reaction of Supply

The mechanism described above presupposes that the supply of a particular commodity is stimulated by higher prices and inhibited by lower prices. In other words, the direct elasticity of supply is positive. If, however, in the case of full employment the total production cannot be expanded, then the expansion of one branch of industry implies the contraction of one or more of all the other branches. It is thus theoretically necessary to set negative indirect elasticities of supply against a positive direct elasticity of supply.

In appendix 2 a consistent system of direct and indirect elasticities of supply is worked out on the assumption that the elasticity of substitution of supply is equal to the average elasticity of substitution for all combinations of products. It follows from this that, just as on the demand side the income elasticity $\mu = 1$ ensures the

7

equality of income and expenditure, so also does the system of supply elasticities guarantee the maintenance of full employment.

Income Effects

In the model assuming complete specialization we have already discussed the effects on nominal income resulting from the abolition of the import duty and the effects on real income, which flow from the influence of price changes.

In the case of incomplete specialization, nominal changes of income, caused by price changes on the production side, occur as additional effects in each of the three phases which we shall again distinguish. There is a change in the price of the imported goods on the import market, and consequently the industries making the same product at home are forced to lower their price too. The result is a drop in the income from production. As a percentage this drop in income is equal to the percentage fall in price times the share which the value of the production in the relevant industry represents in the total expenditure. This share will again be denoted by the symbol q_y. After these prefatory remarks we shall now enter into our discussion of the three phases of the model.

FIRST PHASE

In the first phase we again consider the consequences which the abolition of *all* import duties, i.e. including those imposed on outsiders' products, will have for the countries of the customs union. Since the prices in the import-competing industries fall, these industries will suffer losses as a result of which they will be forced to cut down their production. The production factors thereby released can be put to work in the export industry. The expansion of this industry need not be accompanied by a rise in prices, since the release of production factors from the other industries entails a fall in the price of these factors. As all forces of production continue to be employed, we may conclude that the lowering of income from production is the result of lowering the rate of remuneration of the production factors.

The reaction on the demand side is the same as that described in the model assuming complete specialization, except that the effect of lower prices in the import-competing industries has now also entered into the picture. We shall denote the relative change in income by y.

In the following model we again first calculate the changes in the value of production $(\Delta \bar{X})$ and the changes in nominal expenditure $(\Delta \bar{S})$ and reduce these to the changes in volume. After the foregoing discussion the model for country 1 needs no further commentary. It may be represented as follows:

Model 7.1   First Phase, Abolition of Import Duties.

$$\Delta \bar{X}_1^1 = X_1^1 P_1^1 \left({}_1\bar{\alpha}_1^1 p_1^1 + {}_2\bar{\alpha}_1^1 p_2^1 + {}_3\bar{\alpha}_1^1 p_3^1 \right) \quad \cdots \cdots \quad (1)$$

$$\Delta \bar{X}_2^1 = X_2^1 P_2^1 \left({}_1\bar{\alpha}_2^1 p_1^1 + {}_2\bar{\alpha}_2^1 p_2^1 + {}_3\bar{\alpha}_2^1 p_3^1 \right) \quad \cdots \cdots \quad (2)$$

$$\Delta \bar{X}_3^1 = X_3^1 P_3^1 \left({}_1\bar{\alpha}_3^1 p_1^1 + {}_2\bar{\alpha}_3^1 p_2^1 + {}_3\bar{\alpha}_3^1 p_3^1 \right) \quad \cdots \cdots \quad (3)$$

$$\Delta X_1^1 = \Delta \bar{X}_1^1 - X_1^1 P_1^1 p_1^1 \quad \cdots \cdots \cdots \quad (4)$$

$$\Delta X_2^1 = \Delta \bar{X}_2^1 - X_2^1 P_2^1 p_2^1 \quad \cdots \cdots \cdots \quad (5)$$

$$\Delta X_3^1 = \Delta \bar{X}_3^1 - X_3^1 P_3^1 p_3^1 \quad \cdots \cdots \cdots \quad (6)$$

$$\Delta \bar{S}_1^1 = S_1^1 P_1^1 \left({}_1\bar{\eta}_1^1 p_1^1 + {}_2\bar{\eta}_1^1 p_2^1 + {}_3\bar{\eta}_1^1 p_3^1 + \mu y^1 \right) \quad \cdots \quad (7)$$

$$\Delta \bar{S}_2^1 = S_2^1 P_2^1 \left({}_1\bar{\eta}_2^1 p_1^1 + {}_2\bar{\eta}_2^1 p_2^1 + {}_3\bar{\eta}_2^1 p_3^1 + \mu y^1 \right) \quad \cdots \quad (8)$$

$$\Delta \bar{S}_3^1 = S_3^1 P_3^1 \left({}_1\bar{\eta}_3^1 p_1^1 + {}_2\bar{\eta}_3^1 p_2^1 + {}_3\bar{\eta}_3^1 p_3^1 + \mu y^1 \right) \quad \cdots \quad (9)$$

$$\Delta S_1^1 = \Delta \bar{S}_1^1 - S_1^1 P_1^1 p_1^1 \quad \cdots \cdots \cdots \quad (10)$$

$$\Delta S_2^1 = \Delta \bar{S}_2^1 - S_2^1 P_2^1 p_2^1 \quad \cdots \cdots \cdots \quad (11)$$

$$\Delta S_3^1 = \Delta \bar{S}_3^1 - S_3^1 P_3^1 p_3^1 \quad \cdots \cdots \cdots \quad (12)$$

$$y^1 = q_{y1}^1 p_1^1 + q_{y2}^1 p_2^1 + q_{y3}^1 p_3^1 - q_m^1 t^1 \quad \cdots \cdots \quad (13)$$

$$p_1^1 = 0 \quad \cdots \cdots \cdots \cdots \quad (14)$$

$$p_2^1 = \frac{-t^1}{1 + t^1} \quad \cdots \cdots \cdots \quad (15)$$

$$p_3^1 = \frac{-t^1}{1 + t^1} \quad \cdots \cdots \cdots \quad (16)$$

Numerical Example

As appears from the confrontation tables (page 96) the import duties for country 1 and country 2 in the initial situation are again 20% and 10%, respectively.

In this example we put the elasticity of substitution of supply $\delta = 1$. Using the formulae in appendix 2 we can now immediately calculate the direct and indirect elasticities of supply:

$$_1\bar{\alpha}_1^1 = \quad 1.231 \qquad _2\bar{\alpha}_1^1 = -\, 0.115 \qquad _3\bar{\alpha}_1^1 = -\, 0.115$$
$$_1\bar{\alpha}_2^1 = -\, 0.769 \qquad _2\bar{\alpha}_2^1 = \quad 1.884 \qquad _3\bar{\alpha}_2^1 = -\, 0.115$$
$$_1\bar{\alpha}_3^1 = -\, 0.769 \qquad _2\bar{\alpha}_3^1 = -\, 0.115 \qquad _3\bar{\alpha}_3^1 = \quad 1.884$$

The effect on income of the change in the price of production is

$$(q_{y1}^1 + q_{y2}^1)\,\frac{-\,t^1}{1 + t^1} = \left(\frac{12}{108} + \frac{12}{108}\right)\frac{-\,t^1}{1 + t^1} = -\, 0.0374.$$

Since $q_m^1\, t^1$ is also -0.0374, the total effect on income is -0.075.

For the rest the data are equal to those in the previous chapter: the direct and indirect 'value elasticities' of demand in relation to prices are zero, and the relative price changes are $p_2^1 = p_3^1 = -\, 0.167$. Substitution of these values in model 7.1 leads to the solution given in the following confrontation table.

Country 1

CHANGES AFTER ABOLITION OF IMPORT DUTIES

Resources	Δ Volume	Price	Δ Value	Expend-iture	Δ Volume	Price	Δ Value
X_1^1	$3.06 + 0 =$		3.06	S_1^1	$-4.44 + 0$		$= -4.44$
X_2^1	$-1.53 - 2 =$		-3.53	S_2^1	$2.22 - 4.00$		$= -1.78$
X_3^1	$-1.53 - 2 =$		-3.53	S_3^1	$2.22 - 4.00$		$= -1.78$
T^1			-4.00				
			-8.00				-8.00
M_2^1	$3.75 + 0 =$		3.75	F_1^1	$7.50 + 0$		$= 7.50$
M_3^1	$3.75 + 0 =$		3.75				
			7.50				7.50

In a similar way we can calculate the changes in respect of country 2:

$$\Delta X_1^2 = -\,0.78 \qquad \Delta S_1^2 = \quad 1.15$$

$$\Delta X_2^2 = \quad 1.56 \qquad \Delta S_2^2 = -\,2.30$$

$$\Delta X_3^2 = -\,0.78 \qquad \Delta S_3^2 = \quad 1.15$$

SECOND PHASE

The second phase analyses the consequences of the imposition of the common external tariff. This model makes it even clearer than in the case of complete specialization that our phases cannot be consecutive in terms of time. This is evident, since the adjustment of production requires at the least a term of a few years, and it would therefore be folly to assume that production might first adjust itself to the entire abolition of the import duty, then to the imposition of an external tariff, and finally to the change in the terms of trade designed to produce equilibrium. Our analysis simply gives a new equilibrium towards which the economic quantities tend over a period of years. A more concrete investigation into the process of changing from the one state of equilibrium to the other would call for a more complete dynamic analysis than the author feels capable of undertaking.

After the foregoing, this model offers no further difficulties. As already mentioned (page 84) we shall disregard for simplicity all second-order effects.

Model 7.2   Second Phase, Imposition of External Tariff

$$\Delta X_1^1 = X_1^1\, P_1^1\, {}_3\alpha_1^1\, p_3^1 \quad \cdots \cdots \cdots \cdots \cdots \cdots \quad (1)$$

$$\Delta X_2^1 = X_2^1\, P_2^1\, {}_3\alpha_2^1\, p_3^1 \quad \cdots \cdots \cdots \cdots \cdots \cdots \quad (2)$$

$$\Delta X_3^1 = X_3^1\, P_3^1\, {}_3\alpha_3^1\, p_3^1 \quad \cdots \cdots \cdots \cdots \cdots \cdots \quad (3)$$

$$\Delta S_1^1 = S_1^1\, P_1^1\, ({}_3\eta_1^1\, p_3^1 + \mu\, y^1) \quad \cdots \cdots \cdots \cdots \quad (4)$$

$$\Delta S_2^1 = S_2^1\, P_2^1\, ({}_3\eta_2^1\, p_3^1 + \mu\, y^1) \quad \cdots \cdots \cdots \cdots \quad (5)$$

$$\Delta S_3^1 = S_3^1\, P_3^1\, ({}_3\eta_3^1\, p_3^1 + \mu\, y^1) \quad \cdots \cdots \cdots \cdots \quad (6)$$

$$y^1 = q_{y3}^1\, p_3^1 + q_{m3}^1\, t_3^1 \quad \cdots \cdots \cdots \cdots \cdots \cdots \quad (7)$$

$$p_3^1 = t_3^1 \quad \cdots \cdots \cdots \cdots \cdots \cdots \cdots \quad (8)$$

Numerical Example

For the second phase the elasticities of supply must be calculated afresh, since the value shares of production have changed. There are no further import duties in the initial situation of the second phase, and therefore the prices of the home products competing with imports are equal to unity.

The new elasticities of supply are:

$$_3\alpha_1^1 = -0.10$$

$$_3\alpha_2^1 = -0.10$$

$$_3\alpha_3^1 = 0.90$$

The elasticities of demand would also have to be calculated afresh if the elasticity of substitution of demand were not equal to unity, but since it is, the demand shares remain constant and so therefore do the elasticities of demand.

Next we can calculate the income effect:

$$y^1 = q_{y3}^1 \, p_3^1 + q_{m3}^1 \, t_3^1 = 0.10 \times 0.15 + 0.10 \times 0.15 = 0.03.$$

The change in the price of the imports from outsider countries p_3^1 is is again 0.15. Substitution of these data in model 7.2 gives the changes:

$$\Delta X_1^1 = -1.20 \qquad \Delta X_2^1 = -0.15 \qquad \Delta X_3^1 = 1.35$$

$$\Delta S_1^1 = 1.80 \qquad \Delta S_2^1 = 0.60 \qquad \Delta S_3^1 = -2.40$$

In the same way we can calculate the changes for country 2:

$$\Delta X_1^2 = -0.15 \qquad \Delta X_2^2 = -1.20 \qquad \Delta X_3^2 = 1.35$$

$$\Delta S_1^2 = 0.60 \qquad \Delta S_2^2 = 1.80 \qquad \Delta S_3^2 = -2.40$$

THIRD PHASE

The disequilibrium between supply and demand, which has now appeared after the second phase, is appreciably greater than in the case of complete specialization, since the changes in supply and demand always have the opposite sign, so that an increase in demand is reinforced by a decrease in supply, and vice versa.

The model of the third phase now indicates that, in the state of equilibrium, the sum of the changes in supply must be equal to the sum of the changes in demand. The changes in production resulting from the first and second phases are denoted by ΔX.

Model 7.3 Third Phase, Change in Terms of Trade

$$\Delta X_1 + X_1^1 x_1^1 + X_1^2 x_1^2 + X_1^3 x_1^3 = \Delta S_1 + S_1^1 s_1^1 + $$
$$+ S_1^2 s_1^2 + S_1^3 s_1^3 \quad \cdots \cdots \cdots \cdots \cdots \cdots \cdots \quad (1)$$

$$\Delta X_2 + X_2^1 x_2^1 + X_2^2 x_2^2 + X_2^3 x_2^3 = \Delta S_2 + S_2^1 s_2^1 + $$
$$+ S_2^2 s_2^2 + S_2^3 s_2^3 \quad \cdots \cdots \cdots \cdots \cdots \cdots \cdots \quad (2)$$

$$x_1^1 = {}_1\alpha_1^1 p_1 + {}_2\alpha_1^1 p_2 \quad \cdots \cdots \cdots \cdots \cdots \cdots \quad (3)$$

$$x_1^2 = {}_1\alpha_1^2 p_1 + {}_2\alpha_1^2 p_2 \quad \cdots \cdots \cdots \cdots \cdots \cdots \quad (4)$$

$$x_1^3 = {}_1\alpha_1^3 p_1 + {}_2\alpha_1^3 p_2 \quad \cdots \cdots \cdots \cdots \cdots \cdots \quad (5)$$

$$x_2^1 = {}_1\alpha_2^1 p_1 + {}_2\alpha_2^1 p_2 \quad \cdots \cdots \cdots \cdots \cdots \cdots \quad (6)$$

$$x_2^2 = {}_1\alpha_2^2 p_1 + {}_2\alpha_2^2 p_2 \quad \cdots \cdots \cdots \cdots \cdots \cdots \quad (7)$$

$$x_2^3 = {}_1\alpha_2^3 p_1 + {}_2\alpha_2^3 p_2 \quad \cdots \cdots \cdots \cdots \cdots \cdots \quad (8)$$

$$s_1^1 = {}_1\eta_1^1 p_1 + {}_2\eta_1^1 p_2 + \mu \, (q_{y1}^1 p_1 + q_{y2}^1 p_2) \cdots \cdots \quad (9)$$

$$s_1^2 = {}_1\eta_1^2 p_1 + {}_2\eta_1^2 p_2 + \mu \, (q_{y1}^2 p_1 + q_{y2}^2 p_2) \cdots \cdots \quad (10)$$

$$s_1^3 = {}_1\eta_1^3 p_1 + {}_2\eta_1^3 p_2 + \mu \, (q_{y1}^3 p_1 + q_{y2}^3 p_2) \cdots \cdots \quad (11)$$

$$s_2^1 = {}_1\eta_2^1 p_1 + {}_2\eta_2^1 p_2 + \mu \, (q_{y1}^1 p_1 + q_{y2}^1 p_2) \cdots \cdots \quad (12)$$

$$s_2^2 = {}_1\eta_2^2 p_1 + {}_2\eta_2^2 p_2 + \mu \, (q_{y1}^2 p_1 + q_{y2}^2 p_2) \cdots \cdots \quad (13)$$

$$s_2^3 = {}_1\eta_2^3 p_1 + {}_2\eta_2^3 p_2 + \mu \, (q_{y1}^3 p_1 + q_{y2}^3 p_2) \cdots \cdots \quad (14)$$

Numerical Example

The changes in production and demand resulting from the first and second phases are:

$$\Delta X_1 = \quad 0.93 \qquad \Delta X_2 = -1.32 \qquad \Delta X_3 = \quad 0.39$$

$$\Delta S_1 = -0.89 \qquad \Delta S_2 = \quad 2.32 \qquad \Delta S_3 = -1.43$$

Substitution of equations (3) to (14) in (1) and (2) yields the following two equations containing the price changes as unknown quantities.

$$82p_1 - 41p_2 = -1.82 \qquad p_1 = 0 \qquad \cdots \quad (1a)$$

$$-41p_1 + 82p_2 = \quad 3.64 \qquad p_2 = 0.044 \quad \cdots \quad (2a)$$

As in the example of complete specialization, we can now calculate
the changes in volume which together create equilibrium between
supply and demand in respect of the various commodities:

$$\Delta X_1^1 = -\ 0.36 \qquad \Delta S_1^1 = \quad 0.26 \qquad \Delta F_1^1 = -\ 0.62$$

$$\Delta X_2^1 = \quad 0.40 \qquad \Delta S_2^1 = -\ 0.79 \qquad \Delta M_2^1 = -\ 1.19$$

$$\Delta X_3^1 = -\ 0.04 \qquad \Delta S_3^1 = \quad 0.09 \qquad \Delta M_3^1 = \quad 0.13$$

$$\Delta X_1^2 = -\ 0.36 \qquad \Delta S_1^2 = \quad 0.70 \qquad \Delta M_1^2 = \quad 1.06$$

$$\Delta X_2^2 = \quad 0.71 \qquad \Delta S_2^2 = -\ 0.53 \qquad \Delta F_2^2 = \quad 1.24$$

$$\Delta X_3^2 = -\ 0.35 \qquad \Delta S_3^2 = \quad 0.71 \qquad \Delta M_3^2 = \quad 1.06$$

$$\Delta X_1^3 = -\ 0.04 \qquad \Delta S_1^3 = \quad 0.09 \qquad \Delta M_1^3 = \quad 0.13$$

$$\Delta X_2^3 = \quad 0.40 \qquad \Delta S_2^3 = -\ 0.79 \qquad \Delta M_2^3 = -\ 1.19$$

$$\Delta X_3^3 = -\ 0.36 \qquad \Delta S_3^3 = \quad 0.26 \qquad \Delta F_3^3 = -\ 0.62$$

For the final confrontation table for country 1 and the changes in
imports and exports for the other countries see page 105.

Change in the Exchange Rate

Here again, as in the case of complete specialization, it is possible to
convert the price changes into adjustments of the exchange rate.
As far as foreign relations are concerned, it evidently remains the
same whether one keeps the price level of production constant at a
given percentage change in the exchange rate, or whether the
price level changes by the same percentage with the exchange
rate kept constant. In country 1 the price level has risen by 0.4 %,
in country 2 by 3.6 % and in country 3 by 0.4 %. These countries
can therefore appreciate the value of their currency by these
percentages, but this is a purely nominal manipulation, since the
home market prices in that case must be deflated by the same
percentage. The relative prices on the home-market and home
prices in relation to foreign prices are not thereby affected. With a
view to maintaining a constant price level on the home market it
would naturally be preferable to appreciate the value of the currency
rather than to raise the domestic price level.

FINAL CONFRONTATION TABLE OF
CHANGES IN RESOURCES AND EXPENDITURE

INCOMPLETE SPECIALIZATION

Country 1

Resources	Δ Volume	Δ Price	Δ Value	Expend- iture	Δ Volume	Δ Price	Δ Value
X_1^1	3.06 + 0			S_1^1	— 4.44 + 0		
	— 1.20 + 0				1.80 + 0		
	— 0.36 + 0				0.26 + 0		
	1.50 + 0	=	1.50		— 2.38 + 0	=	— 2.38
X_2^1	— 1.53 — 2.00			S_2^1	2.22 — 4.00		
	0.15 + 0				0.60 + 0		
	0.40 + 0.44				— 0.79 + 0.88		
	— 1.28 — 1.56	=	— 2.84		2.03 — 3.12	=	— 1.09
X_3^1	— 1.53 — 2.00			S_3^1	2.22 — 4.00		
	1.35 + 1.50				— 2.40 + 3.00		
	— 0.04 + 0				0.09 + 0		
	— 0.22 — 0.50	=	— 0.72		— 0.09 — 1.00	=	— 1.09
T^1			— 4.00				
T_3^1			1.50				
			— 4.56				— 4.56
M_2^1	3.31 + 0.44	=	3.75	F_1^1	3.88 + 0	=	3.88
M_3^1	0.13 + 0	=	0.13				
			3.88				3.88

CHANGES OF IMPORTS AND EXPORTS

Country 2

Imports	Δ Volume	Δ Price	Δ Value	Exports	Δ Volume	Δ Price	Δ Value
M_1^2	3.74	+ 0	= 3.74	F_2^2	2.10	+ 0.88	= 2.98
M_3^2	− 0.76	+ 0	= − 0.76				
			2.98				2.98

Country 3

Imports	Δ Volume	Δ Price	Δ Value	Exports	Δ Volume	Δ Price	Δ Value
M_1^3	0.13	+ 0	= 0.13	F_3^3	− 0.62	+ 0	= − 0.62
M_2^3	− 1.19	+ 0.44	= − 0.75				
			− 0.62				− 0.62

Effect on Welfare

The effect on welfare of the changes in the terms of trade, calculated by the two methods indicated in the previous chapter, is here just as little spectacular as in the case of incomplete specialization. Country 1 and country 3 see their welfare fall by 0.4 %, whilst country 2 reaps the benefit of the customs union to the extent of 0.8 % of its real income. Parturiunt montes . . .

However, as stated in chapter IV (page 59) we are not in the first instance concerned with the *effect on specialization* of the tariff removal. However, if we apply the formula given there, we see that the effect on welfare is again particularly meagre. For country 1 the effect on specialization is 0.1 % of the total production, and for country 2 as little as 0.03 %.

Although this result seems improbably small, we find confirmation of our conviction that the effect on specialization is for all practical purposes negligible if we apply to our numerical example Scitovsky's method* for calculating the effect on specialization. We have certain objections to Scitovsky's method, but since we believe that he overestimates the specialization effect, these objections are an argument the more in support of our viewpoint.

Specialization Effect according to Scitovsky

Like ourselves, Scitovsky takes as his basis the increasing marginal cost of production. If country A starts to export more of the *a* commodity, the production of that commodity in country A must be expanded and in country B curtailed. This leads to an increase of marginal cost in country A and to a decrease of marginal cost in country B. There thus exists a positive relation between the ratio of the marginal cost of the *a* commodity in country A with respect to that in country B *and* the exports from country A. The greater the exports from country A the larger will be the ratio of the marginal cost of the *a* commodity in country A to the marginal cost of the *a* commodity in country B.

The same considerations apply to country B: the greater the exports of the *b* commodity from country B the *smaller* will be the ratio of the marginal cost of the *b* commodity in country A to the marginal cost of the *b* commodity in country B. If we denote the marginal costs of the *a* commodity in country A by $_AC_a$, etc., we can represent the situation as Scitovsky ** does in the graph shown in fig. 10.

Equilibrium (E) is achieved where the value of the exports from country A is equal to the value of the exports from country B. We choose our volumes so as to make the prices and marginal cost of both products in both countries equal to unity. Now if country B imposes an ad valorem import duty amounting to $_Bt_a$ on imports from country A, the production of the import-competing industry in country B will be expanded until the

---

* T. Scitovsky, *Economic Theory and Western European Integration*, London (1958) p. 53-68.
**Loc. cit. page 56.

marginal costs of the *a* commodity are t_a per cent higher than those of the *a* commodity in country A. Country B must now produce at higher costs larger amounts of the *a* product, which it would have been able to obtain more cheaply in the other country if no import duty had been imposed. As the figure shows, the loss suffered by country B is not equal to the higher marginal cost of the *a* product times the extra production (= reduced imports) but is equal to only half thereof, or, expressed in a formula:

$$\tfrac{1}{2}\,_Bt_a \times \Delta\,_BM_a.$$

Marginal cost ratio

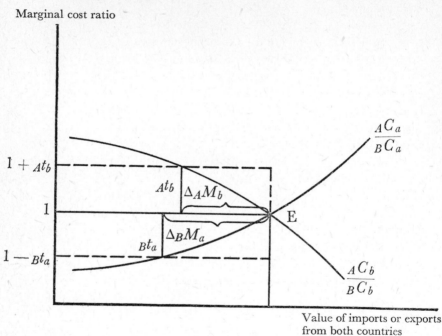

Figure 10. Specialization effect according to Scitovsky

$_AC_a$ = marginal costs of the *a* commodity in country A.
$_At_b$ = ad valorem tariff on the imports of the *b* commodity into country A.
$\Delta\,_BM_a$ = change undergone by the imports of the *a* commodity into country B.

But Scitovsky tells only part of the story, for if the production of the *a* commodity in country B is expanded, the production of the *b* commodity in that country must be contracted, as a result of which the marginal cost of the latter commodity decreases. The loss of production factors in the *a* industry is thus offset by a saving of production factors in the *b* industry *.

Moreover, the production of the *a* commodity in country A must also be cut down. The lower marginal cost in this industry is again partly compensated, however, by the higher marginal cost in the expanding *b* industry, made possible by the fact that country A also imposes a duty on its *b* imports from country B.

The inference is that the total loss in production factors when both parties impose an import duty, and the total gain in production factors when an import duty is abolished, are smaller than calculated by Scitovsky.

Scitovsky further points out that the contraction of trade with the outsiders has an adverse effect in as much as the outsiders (where these countries already impose a duty on imports from the union countries) and also the partner countries are themselves compelled to produce at higher costs the goods which they import in smaller quantities. We shall not go into this question here. At all events, even if we calculate the specialization effect for the purposes of our example by Scitovsky's method, the effect is still only 0.3 % of the total production **.

COMPARISON OF RESULTS

Although a numerical example is nothing but an example, and in itself does not prove much, it is nevertheless interesting to make a comparison between the arithmetical results of the three models discussed, with that of Verdoorn and the models of complete and incomplete specialization.

Strictly speaking a comparison of Verdoorn's results with those of the two other models is not readily possible, because Verdoorn's assumption regarding the elasticity of imports differs from the elasticity of imports which we have implicitly assumed. In our

* Nor does Scitovsky mention that the *domestic demand ratios* are changed by the fact that the *a* product becomes relatively dearer.

**For the method of calculation used, see Scitovsky, op. cit. page 64 ff., where he applies his method to the results of one of Verdoorn's models and finds an effect on specialization amounting to one twentieth per cent of the total production in the relative countries (op. cit. page 67).

CHANGES IN IMPORT PRICES AND IMPORT VOLUMES IN
THE MODELS DISCUSSED, EXPRESSED AS PERCENTAGES
OF THE INITIAL SITUATION

	Verdoorn model	Complete specialization model	Incomplete specialization model
P_1	11.7	— 3.43	0
P_2	18.3	4.13	4.4
M_2^1	4.2	9.1	33.1
M_3^1	10.8	0	1.3
M_1^2	10.9	16.7	37.4
M_3^2	4.1	0	— 7.6
M_1^3	— 0.8	3.4	1.3
M_2^3	— 14.2	— 4.1	— 11.9

opinion, however, it is here that we find the weak point of Verdoorn's model. In his model it makes no difference whether the import share (the share of the value of imports in the value of total expenditure) is large or small.

Although we shall not insist too much on a comparison of our results with those of Verdoorn's model, it may be well to point out that, although in our models the changes in the terms of trade are much smaller than Verdoorn's, the changes in imports are on balance greater than in his case, even in the model of complete specialization, where the supply factors are immaterial. Comparison of the last column with the other confirms our assertion that to disregard the supply factors is to underestimate the changes in imports and exports.

The fact that the changes in the prices of the exported commodities are of only minor significance, both under complete and incomplete specialization, does not entitle one to conclude that their influence on supply is negligible. As regards the structure of supply the home *price ratios* are important, and the changes which they undergo are by no means insignificant.

CHAPTER VIII

THE CUSTOMS UNION
OF THE EUROPEAN ECONOMIC COMMUNITY

Introduction

Having in the previous chapters demonstrated the theoretical implications and the practical operation of the customs union model on the basis of fictitious numerical examples, in this chapter we shall illustrate the operation of the model by taking more realistic figures, relating to the customs union of the European Economic Community.

Now, it is a known fact that, the more general an analysis is, the more heroic are the assumptions one must take. Verdoorn has already made various assumptions which richly deserve that predicate: the assumptions of equal elasticity of substitution of imports and equal elasticity of imports for all countries, and the quantitative value of these elasticities are typical examples.

Since our analysis is even more comprehensive than Verdoorn's, we are compelled to be even bolder. Although we do not assume equal elasticity of imports for all countries, we do assume equal elasticity of substitution of supply and demand and equal elasticity of income for all countries and products. Bolder still is the assumption we must make concerning the nature and size of the various home industries competing with imports.

To this chapter a remark made by W. Arthur Lewis* in another context might well be applied with particular force: 'This is an exercise, and not a prediction'. The object of this chapter is merely to illustrate the theory worked out in the foregoing chapters. A great deal of painstaking statistical research will be needed to lend this exercise the nature of a prediction.

Has this exercise then any 'practical' value? We believe that it has, for theoretical understanding can never be without value in

---

* W. A. Lewis, World Production, Prices and Trade, 1870-1960. *The Manchester School of Economic and Social Studies*. Vol. XX (1952) page 131.

practical dealings, and also because, by varying the assumptions made, we may gain some insight into the possible order of magnitude of the changes that will arise and into the factors that govern these changes.

Limitation of Subject

As the title of this chapter indicates, we shall not discuss the European Economic Community as such but only a part thereof, namely the customs union. It may very well be that the possibility of pursuing a common economic policy and the greater mobility of production factors will appear to be very much more important than the customs union.

Again, in treating the customs union we shall take no account of certain highly important qualitative factors. It is quite possible, and indeed to be hoped, that the mere prospect of the frontiers opening will infuse fresh energy into entrepreneurs. These more qualitative aspects are admirably treated by Viner* and Scitovsky**. We are keenly aware that a customs union, like any other economic reality, does not function so mechanically as our model might possibly suggest.

Another restriction of our subject matter, and one which we must especially emphasize, is that we shall not deal with economic growth. Now the effects of economic growth, seen in the somewhat longer term, are of course quantitatively much more important as regards welfare than the few per cents that result from a customs union. This assertion merely underlines, however, the relative value of our enquiry: there are subjects in the science of economics that are more important than the doctrine of the customs union, but economic growth as such falls outside the scope of this treatise. The customs union may nevertheless influence the *direction* of that growth: as a consequence of the customs union some branches of industry will expand relatively more, others less, or the union may make a certain policy of industrialization desirable. On these problems Verdoorn has a great deal of importance to say.*** It will be

* J. Viner, *The Customs Union Issue*, 1950.
** T. Scitovsky, *Economic Theory and Western European Integration*.
***Prae-advies, p. 95 ff.

enough here to draw attention to these sources without going into the problems concerned.

The Assumptions

We assume full competition. This assumption is not, however, essential to the operation of the model. We might also assume that a certain monopolistic profit margin is imposed on the cost of the products. This margin may of course differ from one product to another, but since we are dealing with very rough aggregates we may assume that the profit margin for all products is equal to the average profit margin.

Regarding the composition of the products it is assumed that the partner countries (the Belgian-Luxembourg Economic Union is considered for convenience as one country) and the outsiders each produce their own product, of which they consume a part themselves and export the remainder. We shall call that product the export product. Each country imports the export product of all other countries, whereas in the models of incomplete specialization it is assumed that these products are also produced in the home countries by the import-competing industries.

A distinction may be made between the home product in the strict sense and the export product. The home product in that sense is neither imported not exported, whereas the export product is sold on the home market as well as being exported. It would certainly be more correct to make this distinction, and it is also possible to build it into the model, but this would simply make the model more complicated without significantly affecting the results. The 'home' product follows the movements of the export product, though to a lesser extent. We have simplified the problem by combining these two products to form an average product.

Regarding the size of the home industries competing with imports, the statistics available are extremely scanty. Attempts made by the author to obtain information in this respect have met with no success. The relative assumptions made here are therefore quite arbitrary. We have assumed two extreme cases. On the one hand we have assumed that the size of the import-competing industries is zero (this is the case of complete specialization), and on the other

8

hand we have deducted the exports from the total production, and of the remainder we have indicated a certain percentage as representing a substitution for imports and divided this equally over the five import products. Other variants could of course be calculated, but we have left it at these two.

Like Verdoorn, we shall take no account of any quantitative restrictions that may exist, and we also follow his example in the treatment of raw materials: we assume that full employment exists before and after the abolition of the import duties, and further that the shifts in the structure of production have no significant effect on the amount of raw materials imported. A consequence of this assumption is that, in the initial situation, disregarding incidental disequilibria, there is no equilibrium in our balance of trade, excluding raw materials. This is immaterial, however, since the balanced adjustment to the customs union implies merely that the *changes* in the value of imports and exports are equal.

The Elasticities

It is clear from the previous chapters that we consider the elasticities of substitution of supply and demand, together with the income elasticity of demand, as the fundamental data from which the other elasticities, in particular the direct and indirect elasticitices of supply and demand, may be deduced. This approach is based on the theoretical notion that the system of direct and indirect elasticities must satisfy certain conditions of consistency: if the income elasticity is unity, the change in expenditure must be equal to the change in income; if the total production remains unaltered, the increase in the production of one commodity must be accompanied by a corresponding decrease in the production of other commodites. Now the given income elasticity equal to unity, and the given elasticities of substitution, are in fact the expression of these fundamental conditions. What is bold about our assumptions from the theoretical point of view is not, therefore, that we regard these elasticities as fundamental, but that we assume the same fundamental elasticities, namely the average, for all commodities and for all countries.

It is perfectly clear that the income elasticity is greater than unity in respect of certain commodities and smaller in respect of others. It is also evident that the substitution between, let us say, steam rollers and cigarettes, is micro-economically unmeasurable, and may be put at zero. This does not alter the fact that macro-economic substitution occurs between investment goods, which include steam rollers, and consumer goods, which include cigarettes. It can broadly be said that the larger and rougher the aggregates the more permissible will it be to work with average income and substitution elasticities. Since our goods are particularly roughly aggregated, we believe that it is permissible by way of approximation to work with average elasticities.

Elasticity of Substitution

The literature on the elasticity of substitution has swollen considerably without any corresponding increase in the practical results.* Most investigations have been extremely partial in their character and they relate mainly to import products of differing origin. Future measurements of these elasticities will undoubtedly remain extremely difficult.

However this may be, the concept of elasticity of substitution can do a great deal to help our understanding of complex economic events. In the absence of more information, however, we are compelled to assume various alternative values for the elasticity of substitution.

As the lowest value of the elasticity of substitution of demand we have chosen $\varphi = 1$, because if the elasticity of substitution were less than unity, the indirect elasticities of demand would be negative, which can be true only for very specific commodities. As a variant we have chosen $\varphi = 4$, which is probably a fairly extreme assumption.

As regards the elasticity of substitution of supply there is an even greater paucity of information. We give here only the value $\delta = 1$ and have calculated a variant for $\delta = 0$.

The Data

It would require too much space to reproduce the data in the form of confrontation tables of resources and expenditure, as we have done in the previous chapters. By way of example we shall present such a confrontation table for the Netherlands, and further confine ourselves to a few tables representing the movement of trade and the structure of production and expenditure. All figures relate to 1956. **

---

* A comprehensive bibliography on this subject is given by I. Morriset: Some Recent Uses of Elasticity of Substitution, *Econometrica*, vol. 21 (1953), pp. 41-62.

** We are greatly indebted to the Economisch Sociologisch Instituut at Tilburg, and particularly to Mr. A. A. J. Smulders, for compiling the data given below and for calculating the average import tariffs.

TABLE 8.1

MOVEMENT OF TRADE IN
SEMI-FINISHED AND END PRODUCTS BETWEEN THE
E.E.C. COUNTRIES MUTUALLY AND WITH OUTSIDERS

(in milliards of U.S. dollars)

to \ from	Netherlands	B.L.E.U.	West Germany	France	Italy	Outsiders
1. Netherlands . . .	—	0.60	0.57	0.10	0.04	1.17
2. B.L.E.U..	0.35	—	0.40	0.25	0.04	0.98
3. West Germany . .	0.40	0.25	—	0.35	0.25	2.61
4. France.	0.15	0.23	0.40	—	0.13	1.24
5. Italy	0.06	0.06	0.30	0.10	—	0.99
6. Outsiders	1.70	1.87	5.53	3.39	1.17	—

Source: *The Network of Intra-european Trade, Trade by Product in 1956*. Paris 1957.
The categories 0, 1 and 2 of the S.I.T.C. were considered as raw materials.

TABLE 8.2

THE STRUCTURE OF PRODUCTION IN THE E.E.C. COUNTRIES

(in milliards of U.S. dollars)

Country \ Commodity	1	2	3	4	5	6
1. Netherlands . . .	5.16	0.20	0.20	0.20	0.20	0.20
2. B.L.E.U..	0.28	6.35	0.28	0.28	0.28	0.28
3. West Germany . .	1.64	1.64	26.31	1.64	1.64	1.64
4. France.	2.08	2.08	2.08	28.49	2.08	2.08
5. Italy	0.96	0.96	0.96	0.96	12.73	0.96

Source: *Statistical Yearbook, 1958*, Table 162. The value of exports has been deducted from the national income less government services. Of the remainder approximately 30 % has been classified as import-competing production and divided equally over the various home products competing with imports.

TABLE 8.3

THE STRUCTURE OF EXPENDITURE IN THE E.E.C. COUNTRIES

(in milliards of U.S. dollars)

Commodity / Country	1	2	3	4	5	6
1. Netherlands . . .	2.50	0.80	0.77	0.30	0.24	1.37
2. B.L.E.U..	0.63	3.34	0.68	0.53	0.32	1.26
3. West Germany . .	2.04	1.89	19.10	1.99	1.89	4.25
4. France.	2.23	2.31	2.48	24.30	2.21	3.32
5. Italy	1.02	1.02	1.26	1.06	11.10	1.95

This table was compiled by adding tables 8.1 and 8.2.

Import Duties

In order to calculate the micro-economic consequences of the customs union for the various branches of industry, it is particularly important to ascertain the level of the import duty which is imposed on the product concerned in the initial situation. This level varies considerably from one product to another. For the purposes of our macro-economic approach, we shall disregard the refinement that it is possible, for example, for the imports from Germany into the Netherlands to carry a heavier average duty than the imports from France. We have thus assumed that each country imposes a uniform tariff on all imported goods, namely the average tariff. This was calculated by taking the arithmetic mean of the existing tariffs for each category of commodities in the Standard International Trade Classification, and by combining these into a weighted mean, the weights being the values of the imports of the various categories. The fact was taken into account that the Benelux countries have already abolished the import tariffs between themselves. As regards the Netherlands and Belgium, the total revenue from the import duties, according to data provided by the Dutch Ministry of Economic Affairs, was divided by the value of imports other than raw materials. See table 8.4 on page 118.

The common external tariff is assumed to be the average of the existing tariffs on imports other than raw materials, namely 12 %. *

---

* Taking into account the imports of raw materials, which are not or scarcely subject to duty, the average value of the common external tariff comes out at roughly 7.5 %.

TABLE 8.4

AVERAGE IMPORT DUTIES OF E.E.C. COUNTRIES

Netherlands . . .	$t^1 = 0.10$
B.L.E.U.	$t^2 = 0.08$
West Germany . .	$t^3 = 0.11$
France.	$t^4 = 0.14$
Italy	$t^5 = 0.19$

Source: For the Netherlands and the B.L.E.U., the Ministry of Economic Affairs. For the other countries: R. Bertrand, *Comparaison du niveau des tarifs douaniers des pays du Marché Commun*, Paris 1958.

Confrontation of Resources and Expenditure

With the aid of the above data we can now draw up for all the countries concerned a confrontation table of resources and expenditure. For the purpose of illustration we shall do this for the Netherlands alone.

Our starting premise is that in the Netherlands the price of the home product and of the B.L.E.U. product, on which no import duties are imposed, are equal to unity, and the prices of the other products competing with imports are $1 + t^1$. The volumes of the latter products are obtained by dividing their value by $1 + t^1$.

As appears from the adjoining confrontation table, the Netherlands in the initial situation has an export surplus. The reason for this is that the Netherlands (like the other E.E.C. countries) imports more raw materials than she exports, and the imports and exports of raw materials are not taken into account.

The Data for the Outsiders

Tables 8.2 and 8.3 do not include the outsiders' structure of production and expenditure. This has been omitted not only because the data are lacking, but also because it would be pointless to attempt to specify the consequences of the customs union on the production and expenditure of such a completely heterogeneous group as the outsiders. Nevertheless, by making a simplified assumption it is possible to round-off the model and determine the effects of the customs union on *trade* with the outsiders.

In the three-country models, dealt with in the previous chapters, the outsiders came on to the stage only in the third act. The first and second phases directly concerned only the partner countries, and the outsiders played merely an indirect part in so far as the demand for the outsiders' product increased or decreased. Although the outsiders participated directly in the third phase, their role was still a secondary one, because the two equilibrium equations relate only to the export products of the union countries (see page 87 and page 103) and not to the export product of the outsiders.

The outsiders played the part of producers and consumers of other countries' products, and thus helped to restore the disturbed balance.

CONFRONTATION TABLE OF RESOURCES AND
EXPENDITURE IN THE INITIAL SITUATION
NETHERLANDS
(in milliards of U.S. dollars)

Resources	Volume	Price	Value	Expend-iture	Volume	Price	Value
X_1^1	5.16	$\times$ 1	= 5.16	S_1^1	2.50	$\times$ 1	= 2.50
X_2^1	0.18	$\times$ 1	= 0.18	S_2^1	0.78	$\times$ 1	= 0.78
X_3^1	0.18	$\times$ 1.1	= 0.20	S_3^1	0.75	$\times$ 1.1	= 0.83
X_4^1	0.18	$\times$ 1.1	= 0.20	S_4^1	0.28	$\times$ 1.1	= 0.31
X_5^1	0.18	$\times$ 1.1	= 0.20	S_5^1	0.22	$\times$ 1.1	= 0.24
X_6^1	0.18	$\times$ 1.1	= 0.20	S_6^1	1.35	$\times$ 1.1	= 1.49
T^1			0.19				
			6.33				6.15
Imports				Exports			
M_2^1	0.60	$\times$ 1	= 0.60	F_1^1	2.66	$\times$ 1	= 2.66
M_3^1	0.57	$\times$ 1	= 0.57				
M_4^1	0.10	$\times$ 1	= 0.10				
M_5^1	0.04	$\times$ 1	= 0.04				
M_6^1	1.17	$\times$ 1	= 1.17				
			2.48				2.66

It may also be said that they fulfilled this task in expanding or reducing their imports, because an increase of expenditure plus a decrease in the production of a home commodity competing with imports is equivalent to an increase in imports.

In our E.E.C. model we have again asigned the same role to the outsiders, but this time we assume that the outsiders will react to changes in the prices of the products imported from the E.E.C. countries in accordance with the partial elasticities of imports. In so doing, we thus partly abandon the *total* analysis and confine ourselves to a partial analysis as far as the outsiders are concerned. In their respect we apply Verdoorn's method, but we assume that the import shares (as defined by Verdoorn) in the total imports of the outsiders are so small as to be negligible. In that case the partial elasticities of imports are equal to the share elasticity *.

We have chosen a value of -2 for the outsiders' partial elasticity of imports, in accordance with the common assumption made in regard to the export elasticity of the Netherlands. We have also calculated a variant for the value -4.

Data under Complete Specialization

It is scarcely necessary to recapitulate all the data for the case of complete specialization. The interested reader will be able to construe them himself. Since there is no home industry competing with imports in this case, all values per line in the production matrix (table 8.2) have been added together and placed in the main diagonal. The expenditure matrix (table 8.3) has in its main diagonal the value of the total production per country minus the value of the exports, and for the rest the value of expenditure is equal to the value of imports plus import duty.**

The Models

The operation of the models and the method of calculation have been explained in the previous chapters at sufficient length to allow as to dispense with an explanation of the even more complicated six-country model. In appendix 4 the models of complete and incomplete specialization are represented in symbolic form.

Presentation of Results

The confrontation of changes in resources and expenditure is undoubtedly the most lucid method of presenting the results. Lack of space, however, prevents us from including all the confrontation tables. We shall there-

---

* We may write, for example, $m_1^6 = {_1}e_1^6\,p_1 + {_2}e_1^6\,p_2 + \ldots + {_5}e_1^6\,p_5 = \beta\,p_1$, if the import shares are zero. See page 67 and P. J. Verdoorn, *Prae-advies*, pp. 119-120.

** For comparison see the initial confrontation tables for complete and incomplete specialization in the three-country models (page 79 and page 96).

fore, again by way of example, present the confrontation for the Netherlands of the variant: incomplete specialization where the elasticities of substitution of demand and of supply are equal to unity ($\delta = 1$ and $\varphi = 1$, respectively) and the partial elasticity of imports for the outsiders (for convenience denoted by β) is -2.

As in the previous chapters, the confrontation data are arrived at by adding together the results of the three separate phases. They show how the changes in imports and exports under incomplete specialization are caused by the reaction of demand as well as the reaction of supply to the autonomous and induced price changes. As a result, even where the values of the fundamental elasticities are moderate, marked changes take place in the imports and exports from and to the various countries, although the changes in the total imports and exports are, on balance, not particularly great, namely 11 % and 5 %. The latter is due to the part played by the import products from B.L.E.U. and from outsider countries; for while all other import products on the home market become cheaper, the price of the Belgian-Luxembourg product rises by 6 %, and the outsiders' product also becomes ultimately dearer, since the external tariff is 2 % higher than the existing tariff. The fact that the imports from the outsider countries nevertheless increase is attributable to income and substitution effects.

As we have said, it is not feasible to reproduce all the results in confrontation tables of resources and expenditure. We have therefore drawn up from the comparative data for the principal variants a matrix of the changes in the volumes of trade, which will be found in tables 8.5 to 8.8.

Changes in Imports and Exports

As we have made clear in the foregoing, we are entirely aware that the assumption of complete specialization, which excludes the supply factors, is not realistic. Nevertheless, two variants have been worked out for this assumption in order to make a comparison possible with the models of incomplete specialization. As was to be expected, the import variations in the two models of complete specialization are roughly proportional to the value of the elasticity of substitution. This is not so, however, as regards the changes in relation to the outsiders, because the partial elasticity of imports in their case was not varied.

By contrast, the differences between the cases of complete and incomplete specialization are much greater. The changes found, even where moderate assumptions are made in regard to the elasticities, are substantially greater than those calculated by Verdoorn, but in view of the changes that actually occur in trade, which of

CONFRONTATION TABLE OF CHANGES IN RESOURCES AND EX-
PENDITURE RESULTING FROM THE CUSTOMS UNION OF THE E.E.C.

NETHERLANDS

(Millions of U.S. dollars and percentage change in volumes)

Resources	Δ Volume	Δ Price	Δ Value	Expend-iture	Δ Volume	Δ Price	Δ Value
X_1^1 85	(1.6)	+ 279	= 364	S_1^1 –53	(– 2.1)	+ 135	= 82
X_2^1 3	(1.6)	+ 9	= 12	S_2^1 –15	(– 1.9)	+ 40	= 25
X_3^1 –25	(–13.7)	– 18	= –43	S_3^1 98	(13.0)	– 76	= 22
X_4^1 –30	(–16.5)	– 23	= –53	S_4^1 44	(15.6)	– 37	= 7
X_5^1 –27	(–14.8)	– 23	= –50	S_5^1 31	(14.0)	– 30	= 1
X_6^1 – 5	(– 2.7)	+ 4	= – 1	S_6^1 20	(1.5)	+ 26	= 46
T^1			–187				
T_6^1			141				
			183				183

Imports				Exports			
M_2^1 –18	(– 3.0)	+ 37	= 19	F_1^{12} –12	(– 3.4)	+ 21	= 9
M_3^1 123	(21.6)	+ 4	= 127	F_1^{13} 110	(27.5)	+ 25	= 135
M_4^1 74	(74.0)	– 2	= 72	F_1^{14} 124	(82.7)	+ 9	= 133
M_5^1 58	(145.0)	+ 0	= 58	F_1^{15} 129	(215.0)	+ 3	= 132
M_6^1 25	(2.1)	+ 0	= 25	F_1^{16} –213	(–12.5)	+ 106	= –107
			302				302

TABLE 8.5

CUSTOMS UNION OF THE E.E.C.

CHANGES IN THE VOLUME OF INTERNATIONAL TRADE

Complete specialization $\varphi = 1, \beta = -2$

to \ from	Netherlands	B.L.E.U.	West Germany	France	Italy	Outsiders	Total imports
Millions of U.S. dollars 1956							
Netherlands . .	—	— 5	53	11	6	—20	45
B.L.E.U. . . .	1	—	33	26	5	—27	38
West Germany	41	25	—	44	38	—11	138
France	17	25	46	—	21	6	115
Italy	8	8	40	15	—	21	91
Outsiders . . .	—43	—54	—108	65	84	—	—56
Total exports .	23	— 1	64	161	153	—30	—
Percentage changes							
Netherlands . .	—	— 1	9	11	14	— 1	2
B.L.E.U. . . .	0	—	8	10	13	— 3	2
West Germany	10	10	—	13	15	0	4
France	11	11	12	—	16	1	5
Italy	13	13	13	15	—	2	6
Outsiders . . .	— 3	— 3	— 2	2	7	—	0
Total exports .	1	0	1	4	9	0	—

TABLE 8.6

CUSTOMS UNION OF THE E.E.C.

CHANGES IN THE VOLUME OF INTERNATIONAL TRADE

Complete specialization $\varphi = 4$, $\beta = -2$

to \ from	Netherlands	B.L.E.U.	West Germany	France	Italy	Outsiders	Total imports
Millions of U.S. dollars 1956							
Netherlands . .	—	—29	211	48	24	—56	200
B.L.E.U. . . .	— 7	—	129	109	23	—93	161
West Germany	155	97	—	185	164	— 4	597
France	60	92	171	—	87	13	423
Italy	27	27	145	60	—	64	323
Outsiders . . .	—77	—86	—172	86	104	—	—145
Total exports .	159	100	484	488	402	—75	—
Percentage changes							
Netherlands . .	—	— 5	37	48	61	— 5	8
B.L.E.U. . . .	— 2	—	33	44	57	— 9	9
West Germany	39	37	—	53	67	0	16
France	40	40	43	—	67	1	20
Italy	46	45	48	60	—	6	21
Outsiders . . .	— 5	— 5	— 3	3	9	—	— 1
Total exports .	6	3	6	12	25	— 1	—

TABLE 8.7

CUSTOMS UNION OF THE E.E.C.

CHANGES IN THE VOLUME OF INTERNATIONAL TRADE

Incomplete specialization $\varphi = 1, \delta = 1, \beta = -2$

to \ from	Netherlands	B.L.E.U.	West Germany	France	Italy	Outsiders	Total imports
Millions of U.S. dollars 1956							
Netherlands . .	—	—18	123	74	59	24	263
B.L.E.U. . . .	—12	—	111	113	73	7	292
West Germany	110	112	—	384	323	—141	792
France	124	134	358	—	379	—124	871
Italy	129	132	253	274	—	45	831
Outsiders . . .	—213	—227	—73	138	12		—304
Total exports .	138	133	772	983	846	—190	—
Percentage changes							
Netherlands . .	—	— 3	22	74	147	1	11
B.L.E.U. . . .	— 3	—	28	45	184	0	16
West Germany	28	45	—	110	129	— 1	21
France	83	58	90	—	292	— 1	41
Italy	214	219	84	274	—	1	55
Outsiders . . .	—13	—12	0	0	0	—	— 3
Total exports .	5	4	11	23	52	— 3	—

TABLE 8.8

CUSTOMS UNION OF THE E.E.C.

CHANGES IN THE VOLUME OF INTERNATIONAL TRADE

Incomplete specialization $\varphi = 4$, $\delta = 1$, $\beta = -2$

to \ from	Netherlands	B.L.E.U.	West Germany	France	Italy	Outsiders	Total imports
Millions of U.S. dollars 1956							
Netherlands . .	—	—120	360	190	140	90	660
B.L.E.U. . . .	—80	—	310	310	180	0	720
West Germany	260	270	—	1030	860	—280	2140
France	270	310	900	—	970	—240	2210
Italy	290	310	650	690	—	180	2120
Outsiders . . .	—260	—270	—210	90	—10	—	—660
Total exports .	490	510	2040	2310	2140	—250	—
Percentage changes							
Netherlands . .	—	—20	63	190	350	8	27
B.L.E.U. . . .	—23	—	78	124	450	0	24
West Germany	65	108	—	294	344	—11	30
France	180	135	225	—	746	—19	53
Italy	483	517	217	690	—	18	130
Outsiders . . .	—15	—14	— 4	3	— 1	—	— 5
Total exports .	18	17	28	55	131	— 4	—

course are governed by many other factors too, they do not appear to be unrealistic.

It should be noted, however, that a consequence of our assumption concerning the various home industries competing with imports is that the percentage change in relatively small imports (e.g. in the imports from the Netherlands in Italy) is greater than in relatively large imports. This is evident, since we have assumed that the size of the competitive home industries is equal for all import goods. The same change in production (and in expenditure) thus gives rise to a greater percentage change in the imports of the product which has a low import share. Even so, this assumption does not seem more unrealistic than another assumption one might make, namely that the home industry competing with imports is proportional in size to the import share. We can only regret that there are no data to show whether this is in fact the case.

We may conclude, however, that in spite of the substantial percentage changes which occur in trade between the individual countries, the changes in the total volume of imports and exports — disregarding the more extreme case of incomplete specialization where $\varphi = 4$ — are not particularly marked, especially when one bears in mind that the consequences of the customs union extend over 10 to 20 years.

Changes in Terms of Trade

The changes in the terms of trade of the E.E.C. countries in relation to the outsiders, calculated for six variants, are presented in table 8.9.

As can be seen, it is above all the structure of supply and demand that influences the changes in the terms of trade. The dividing line in the order of magnitude of the changes is found between complete and incomplete specialization, but it is not only the changes in supply that bring about the greater changes in the terms of trade, for even if the elasticity of supply is zero under incomplete specialization, the changes are still greater than under complete specialization. We may therefore conclude that the magnitude of the elasticities of substitution has relatively little influence on the magnitude of the change in the terms of trade. On the other hand, these elas-

TABLE 8.9

PERCENTAGE CHANGES IN THE TERMS OF TRADE
OF THE E.E.C. COUNTRIES VIS A VIS OUTSIDERS

	Complete specialization		Incomplete specialization			
	$\beta = -2$		$\beta = -2$			$\beta = -4$
	$\varphi = 1$	$\varphi = 4$	$\varphi = 1$ $\delta = 1$	$\varphi = 1$ $\delta = 0$	$\varphi = 4$ $\delta = 1$	$\varphi = 1$ $\delta = 1$
Netherlands	1.3	2.3	6.3	5.1	7.5	4.7
B.L.E.U.	1.4	2.3	6.1	5.0	7.2	4.5
West Germany . . .	1.0	1.5	0.7	0.9	1.9	0.2
France	—1.0	—1.3	—2.4	—1.8	—1.3	—2.1
Italy	—3.6	—4.4	—0.5	—0.6	0.2	—0.9

ticities, and in particular the elasticity of substitution of supply, have a considerable influence on the magnitude of the changes in imports.*

Changes in the Structure of Production

In the unrealistic case of complete specialization, there will be no change in the structure of production. Under incomplete specialization, however, production will undergo a displacement. The home industries competing with imports are in part supplanted, whilst the production of the 'home' product is expanded. As we have seen, however (page 113) this 'home' product is an average of the home trade industry and the export industry, though the change will obviously be felt more keenly in the export sector of the 'home' product. In the table below, the percentage change of the 'home' products is thus an underestimated indication of the changed production in the pure export industry. The changes for the variant $\varphi = 4$ do not differ significantly from the values given here.

* The changes in imports and exports under incomplete specialization, at $\varphi = 1$, $\delta = 0$, amount to roughly half the changes occurring at $\varphi = 1$, $\delta = 1$.

TABLE 8.10

PERCENTAGE CHANGES IN THE
PRODUCTION STRUCTURE OF THE E.E.C. COUNTRIES

Incomplete specialization $\delta = 1$, $\varphi = 1$

Country \ Commodity	1	2	3	4	5	6
Netherlands	1.6	—1.4	—13.8	—16.4	—15.0	—2.5
B.L.E.U.	—1.7	1.6	—11.7	—14.5	—14.7	0
West Germany . . .	—3.6	—3.8	1.6	—11.9	—12.2	3.0
France	—3.6	—3.8	— 9.1	1.6	—12.2	3.0
Italy	—8.3	—8.5	—13.8	—16.6	3.2	—2.5

The Outsiders

As we have seen (page 92) the changes in the terms of trade of the E.E.C. countries in relation to the outsiders depend to a very marked extent on the level of the external tariff. Disregarding second-order effects, we can find a linear relation between the changes that occur in the terms of trade at different levels of the external tariff.* This relation can be represented in a graph, and by way of example we give here the graphic representation for the variant $\varphi = 1$; $\delta = 1$; $\beta = -2$.

The graph really shows that the outsiders definitely need not suffer any disadvantage from the customs union. On the contrary, if the external tariff is fixed too low, the Community as a whole will see its terms of trade deteriorate, and will thus, to its own detriment, gratuitously benefit the welfare of the outsiders.

* Where the external tariff is low, the changes in volume resulting from the second phase (imposition of external tariff) will be proportionately smaller. Consequently, the constants in the five final equations will also be smaller. By solving these five equations for two values of the external tariff, we find, for each change in the terms of trade, the values with which we can indicate the linear relationship.

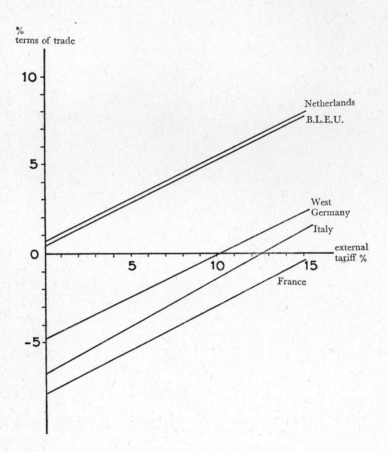

Figure 11 Relation between external tariff and terms of trade

$$\varphi = 1, \delta = 1, \beta = -2$$

The Effect on Welfare

The effect of the customs union on welfare can be resolved into the effects which the change in the terms of trade and the change in specialization have on real income (see page 91 and page 106). The advantage of improved terms of trade lies in the fact that more goods become available through imports than must be forgone in exports. Since these differences are already known (see tables 8.5 — 8.8) the simplest way to calculate the increased welfare resulting from the changed terms of trade is to divide the import surplus per country by the volume of the total expenditure. This has been done in table 8.11.

TABLE 8.11

INCREASED REAL INCOME OF E.E.C. COUNTRIES AS A RESULT
OF CHANGED TERMS OF TRADE WHEN AN EXTERNAL
TARIFF OF 12 % IS IMPOSED

(percentage of the volume of expenditure)

	Complete specialization		Incomplete specialization	
	$\varphi = 1$	$\varphi - 4$	$\varphi = 1$ $\delta = 1$	$\varphi = 4$ $\delta = 1$
Netherlands . . .	0.39	0.72	2.28	3.00
B.L.E.U.	0.60	0.94	2.44	3.22
West Germany .	0.25	0.38	0.07	0.33
France	—0.13	—0.13	—0.32	—0.28
Italy	—0.38	—0.48	—0.09	—0.12

The Belgian-Luxembourg Economic Union and the Netherlands, the countries which were least protectionist in the initial situation, will have the most advantage, West Germany will remain roughly the same, whilst France and Italy will suffer with the outsiders a slight loss. More conspicuous than this sequence is the order of magnitude of the changes. Spread over ten to twenty years they are in fact entirely negligible. One might infer from this that the customs union *in itself* is scarcely worth the effort to achieve it, but also that *if* the customs union is a necessary component of really fruitful cooperation, then neither the outsiders nor France and Italy have much reason to be apprehensive of its results.

Besides the influence of the terms of trade on welfare, however, we still have to consider the production gain or the effect on specialization resulting from the reduced protectionism. After what has been said on the subject in the previous chapters, it is unlikely that this effect will be at all appreciable. The most promising case, namely that of Italy under incomplete specialization at $\varphi = 4$, $\delta = 1$, shows a production gain of less than 0.1 per cent, calculated by our method (see page 59). But even if the specialization effect be calculated by Scitovsky's method, which, as we have indicated (page 107) involves in our opinion an over-estimation, the production gain in the most extreme case is still less than 0.4 %.

We may therefore conclude that the customs union in itself has a negligible influence on welfare.

CHAPTER IX

SUMMARY AND CONCLUSIONS

Professor Tinbergen once said that, in view of the alarming amount of economic literature constantly appearing, every writer ought to provide a short summary of his ideas and should indicate what he believes to be the new aspect of his contribution. Tinbergen himself has set the example on several occasions.* Now that we have taken it upon ourselves to plant yet another sapling in the forest of literature on international economic relations, we shall gladly follow his precept and endeavour to summarize the contents of our book with the salient conclusions.

We believe that any value this book may have resides in the fact that an effort is made here to present a general equilibrium model in which the theory of prices is consistently worked out. Under the influence of the Keynesian school, the price theory has fallen somewhat into discredit. The Keynesians have placed so much emphasis on the analysis of employment that they have virtually ignored the function of prices. One might also say, perhaps, that they have been so fascinated by macro-economics that they have shown little interest in a synthesis of micro and macro economics. In our belief, however, to neglect the theory of prices is to impoverish economic science and in some degree to imperil economic policy.

In the first chapters of this book the theoretical foundation was laid for the subsequent equilibrium models. We took as our basis the doctrine of prices and production as set forth by Professor Schouten in his book 'Exacte Economie'. The theorems of comparative costs, for instance, were worked out with the aid of transformation lines and demand curves. Our procedure followed the method of diminishing abstraction, and we confined ourselves in the first instance to two-country, two-product models. In regard to demand, we assumed that the elasticity of substitution was

---

* E.g. *International Economic Integration*, Amsterdam 1954.

equal to unity, thus implying constant expenditure shares. This enabled us in particular to treat systematically the influence of the supply factors on international trade.

First of all, it was assumed that labour was the only scarce production factor. The transformation line for labour then gives the autarkic costs and price ratios per country, which constitute the extreme limit of the terms of trade on the international market. By means of graphs and using a simple mathematical model, we explained the theorem of comparative costs and indicated the method of determining the volume of international trade and the terms of trade. It was also possible to establish the limits of complete specialization. We thereby arrived at the not-unfamiliar conclusion that incomplete specialization is more probable than complete specialization the more the countries involved differ in size, the less is the demand for the product of the small country and the lower are the relative differences in costs.

We then widened our scope by assuming that capital was scarce as well as labour. This provided the opportunity to examine the significance of curved transformation lines by treating the transitional case in which only a few technologies are known per product. It was thereby demonstrated that the relative cost ratio is not constant, but depends on the structure of production, and vice versa. This point was important for our later proposition that a change in price ratio gives rise to a change in the structure of production, since the economic exchange-ratio of the products must correspond to the technical ratio of substitution. Finally, the mechanism of equilibrium in international trade was demonstrated. Under free trade, equilibrium arises when the marginal cost ratio in both countries is equal and when supply and demand are in equilibrium with one another. As a curiosity, it was shown that, where economies of scale exist, international trade in fact creates differences in comparative costs, which lead to complete specialization.

So much, then, for the first two chapters. In practical terms they offer little of novelty, but perhaps there may be something new in the method of presentation, particularly in the verbal, graphic and symbolic treatment of the subject matter, followed by a numerical example. The next two chapters examine the ways in which international trade is affected by the imposition of import duties. In the third chapter the supply factors were disregarded, and the case of complete specialization was discussed.

In the first place the imposition of import duties changes the price ratio, and hence the demand ratios in the country which imposes the duty. Since supply under complete specialization remains unaffected, the changes lead to disequilibrium in the relation between supply and demand. Equilibrium must be restored by relatively increasing the price of the commodity which has, in the first instance, become relatively cheaper. We referred to this price increase as the change in the terms of trade designed to create equilibrium. The transition from the original state of equilibrium to the new one was then analysed in two phases: the disturbance of equilibrium due to the imposition of the import duty, and the restoration of equilibrium by changing the terms of trade.

In the third chapter we also discussed for the first time the significance of the elasticities and their mutual relationship, although the derivation of the latter, in view of its technicalities, is left to the appendices. The idea of the mutual relations between the fundamental and the derived elasticities is not new,* although there is, we believe, something new in our method of deducing them and in the calculated relations between the elasticities of supply**.

In a survey of recent contributions to the theory of international economic relations, M. van Meerhaeghe*** has drawn attention to the need for better integration of income and price effects in the explanation of the balance of payments equilibrium. We believe that our models, and in particular the part played in them by the income

---

* See: Allen and Hicks, A Reconsideration of the Theory of Value, *Economica*, vol. I, 1934, p. 196-220. Also C. E. V. Leser, Die Konstruktion eines Systems von Konsumfunktionen mit Hilfe von Annahmen über die Substitutionselastizitäten. *IFO-Studien*, 5, 1959 pp. 39-65.

** We gladly acknowledge, however, our indebtedness in this connection to Prof. Schouten.

****Recente bijdragen tot de theorie der internationale economische betrekkingen,* Ghent 1959, page 94. For a review of the literature dealing with income and price effects, see pp. 55-60.

elasticity, make a modest contribution to that integration. Our approach, which is in essence neo-classical, depends on Say's law which states that, in the somewhat longer term, income must be equal to expenditure. We have given substance to this law by postulating that the macro-economic elasticity of income must be unity, for the whole income will then be spent and not more than the whole income. Now price changes, apart from their effects on the structure of supply and demand (substitution effects) also have their effects on income. A price increase, for example, implies a fall in real income, nominal income remaining constant; on the other hand it causes a rise in the nominal income from production. In a closed economy, these effects will compensate one another. In an open economy, where the demand for a particular commodity is not equal to the home production of that commodity, this will not be the case.

By now deriving our direct and indirect elasticities of demand from the income and substitution elasticities, and by consistently relating all the effects of price changes on income to the income elasticities of demand, which we put equal to unity, we arrive at a new equilibrium in the balance of payments which takes account of the substitution effects and of the income effects of autonomous price changes.

Finally, in chapter 3 we considered the concept of prohibitive import duties and examined the change brought about in the terms of trade by the imposition of import duties. It was shown that under complete specialization, non-prohibitive duties mutually imposed on imports have scarcely any influence on welfare, whereas the improvement in the terms of trade of a country which imposes a tariff unilaterally is greater the smaller is the value share of imports in that country.

In chapter 4 the models of the previous chapter were extended by the inclusion of supply factors. The general model was then reduced to an import and export model. This was done to enable us to say more about the concept of the elasticity of imports and its corollary, the elasticity of exports. Just as the import and export model was derived from the general model, so too is the elasticity of imports a highly complex quantity, dependent on the elasticities of substitution of supply and demand, on the income elasticity and on the structure of supply and demand. The derivation of these import and export elasticities for the two-country model is given in appendix 3, where moreover the not uninteresting conclusion is drawn that the absolute value of the elasticity of imports is always greater than or at any rate equal to unity. This case, then, always satisfies the Marshall-Lerner condition, which states that a devaluation has a favourable effect on the balance of payments only when the sum of the elasticities of imports and exports is greater than unity. The highly complex nature of the import and export elasticities led us to the conclusion that Marshall's reciprocal demand curves really conceal more than they disclose.

At the end of the fourth chapter an attempt was made to determine by approximation the 'production loss' consequent upon protectionism, and the 'production gain' or the specialization effect resulting from reduced protection. The values found were small, even smaller than the already minute specialization effect found by Scitovsky. Incidentally, it is shown later on, in chapter 7, that Scitovsky's specialization effect contains an over-estimation.

After thus having applied our method to the theory of free trade and protection, we arrived at the principal subject of this book, namely the customs union. The fifth chapter is entirely devoted to Verdoorn's interesting approach, which indeed prompted the writing of this book. Notwithstanding our admiration of the author, some criticism is made of his approach. We believe, for example, that we have shown his assumption of equal elasticity of imports *and* equal share elasticity to be contradictory, because given an equal share elasticity for all countries and all products, which in our view is equivalent to the elasticity of substitution of demand, the elasticity of imports must differ from one country to the other. Moreover, we believe that the elasticity of imports must always be greater than unity and not, as Verdoorn assumes, 0.5. Criticism is also made of the absence of supply factors in his model, and it is pointed out that his partial approach does not do justice to the shifts in demand on the home market.

In chapters six and seven we explain the operation of our own general equilibrium model, applicable to the cases of complete and

incomplete specialization, respectively. These are comparative statistical models, which analyse the transition from the original
state of equilibrium to the new state of equilibrium in three phases,
namely the consequences of the abolition of all import duties, the
consequences of imposing the external tariff, and finally the
restoration of equilibrium by adjustments in the terms of trade.
With the aid of these models, which imply equilibrium in the
balance of payments and full employment in the initial and final
situations, we calculated not only the changes in the terms of trade
but also the changes in production and real expenditure, and hence
the changes in imports and exports. Our break here with the
traditional two-country models of international trade does, in our
opinion, offer something new, even though the way was paved by
the work of Verdoorn.*

Whilst Verdoorn chose an adjustment of the rate of exchange as
the instrument designed to restore equilibrium in his model, we
have used in our models the adjustment of export prices. A simple
method is given, however, of converting these price changes into
changes in the exchange rates.

The magnitude of the change in the terms of trade is shown to
depend on the extent to which the countries were protectionist
before the introduction of the customs union, and further on the
level of the external tariff. It is indicated that it is always possible
to have an external tariff which does not reduce the outsiders'
terms of trade, but that an unduly low external tariff impairs the
terms of trade of the customs union as a whole in relation to the
outsiders.

In the eighth chapter our models are applied to the customs
union of the European Economic Community. It is pointed out,
in the words of W. A. Lewis, that this is an exercise and not a
prediction, since the statistics available are so sadly inadequate.
Not only is little known about the magnitude of the elasticities of
substitution, but scarcely any investigation has been made con-

---

*   H. Makower and G. Morton, in an article entitled: A Contribution towards
    a Theory of Customs Union, *The Economic Journal*, Vol. LXIII, 1953, pp.
    33-49, also give multi-country models, but their object is more restricted.

cerning the size of the home industry competing with imports, a factor of particular importance for our models. If this book were able to convince statisticians of the value of enquiries along these lines, we believe our work would have served a useful purpose. For it is plain that the size of the competitive home industry has a very pronounced influence on the changes in imports and exports resulting from the customs union.

In the absence of the fundamental data we have had to confine ourselves to presenting the results that emerge from various alternative assumptions. These results are collected in a number of tables in chapter eight. The Netherlands, and the Belgian-Luxembourg Economic Union, the countries that were least protectionist in the initial situation, are shown to derive the greatest benefit; Italy and France suffer a slight setback, whereas West Germany and the outsiders are for all practical purposes no better or worse off than before.

The effect on specialization, in whatever way it may be calculated, is extremely slight, and in any case smaller than half a per cent of the total production of the E.E.C. countries. We therefore arrived at the conclusion that the advantages of the customs union *in itself* scarcely justify, if at all, the painful and by no means easy process of adjustment which it entails. It is possible, however, that the other advantages of broader international cooperation in the E.E.C. are so considerable as to demand the creation of the customs union as a necessary component of that cooperation.

One last remark. The general equilibrium model given here may also be used in another way, for example in order to develop the theory of cost-inflationary taxes and of price-deflationary subsidies. For the model shows how autonomous price changes affect the whole structure of supply and demand, and not merely the supply and demand in respect of products which are taxed or subsidized. Here again, however, in the present state of economic science, and in particular having regard to the lack of statistical data, such a model will serve more to deepen our theoretical insight than to help us arrive at predictions.

APPENDIX 1

DERIVATION OF ELASTICITIES OF DEMAND

The models make use of direct and indirect elasticities of demand. Since only the elasticities of substitution of demand and the income elasticity are assumed to be given, it is necessary to determine the relation between the various elasticities*.

The elasticity of substitution of demand, denoted by φ, indicates by what percentage the demand ratio between two products rises or falls if their price ratio rises or falls by 1 %. Expressed as a formula:

$$\frac{d\dfrac{S_1}{S_2}}{\dfrac{S_1}{S_2}} : \frac{d\dfrac{P_1}{P_2}}{\dfrac{P_1}{P_2}} \equiv -\varphi \quad \ldots \ldots \ldots \ldots \quad (1)$$

Since $\quad d\dfrac{S_1}{S_2} = \dfrac{S_2\, d\, S_1 - S_1\, d\, S_2}{(S_2)^2}$

and $\quad d\dfrac{P_1}{P_2} = \dfrac{P_2\, d\, P_1 - P_1\, d\, P_2}{(P_2)^2},$

we may reduce (1) to:

$$s_1 - s_2 \equiv -\varphi_{12}\,(p_1 - p_2) \quad \ldots \ldots \ldots \ldots \quad (1a)$$

(Capital letters denote absolute values, small letters relative deviations.)

The complete set of equations defining the elasticities of substitution relating to the demand for product 1 is as follows:

$$\begin{aligned}
s_1 - s_2 &\equiv -\varphi_{12}\,(p_1 - p_2) \\
s_1 - s_3 &\equiv -\varphi_{13}\,(p_1 - p_3) \\
s_1 - s_n &\equiv -\varphi_{1n}\,(p_1 - p_n) \quad \ldots \ldots \ldots \ldots \quad (2)
\end{aligned}$$

Multiplying both sides by the corresponding value share gives:

$$\begin{aligned}
q_{s2}\,(s_1 - s_2) &= -q_{s2}\,\varphi_{12}\,(p_1 - p_2) \\
q_{s3}\,(s_1 - s_3) &= -q_{s3}\,\varphi_{13}\,(p_1 - p_2) \\
q_{sn}\,(s_1 - s_n) &= -q_{sn}\,\varphi_{1n}\,(p_1 - p_n) \quad \ldots \ldots \ldots \quad (3)
\end{aligned}$$

* In this connection see also F. de Roos and D. B. J. Schouten, *Groeitheorie*, Haarlem 1960, Appendix, to whom we are indebted for the following derivations.

After summation, (3) becomes:

$$(q_{s2} + q_{s3} + \ldots + q_{sn})\, s_1 - q_{s2}\, s_2 - q_{s3}\, s_3 - \ldots -$$
$$- q_{sn}\, s_n = - (q_{s2}\, \varphi_{12} + q_{s3}\, \varphi_{13} + \ldots + q_{sn}\, \varphi_{1n})\, p_1 +$$
$$+ q_{s2}\, \varphi_{12} p_2 + \ldots + q_{sn}\, \varphi_{1n} p_n \cdot \ldots \ldots \ldots \ldots \quad (4)$$

Since the sum of the value shares is unity, (4) becomes:

$$s_1 - (q_{s1}\, s_1 + q_{s2}\, s_2 + \ldots + q_{sn}\, s_n) = - (q_{s2} \varphi_{12} + \ldots +$$
$$+ q_{sn}\, \varphi_{1n})\, p_1 + q_{s2}\, \varphi_{12} p_2 + \ldots + q_{sn}\, \varphi_{1n} p_n \cdot \ldots \ldots \quad (5)$$

If we disregard all income effects, the total expenditure remains unchanged and therefore the weighted sum of the relative changes is equal to zero. As we are considering the substitution effect only, we assume income to be constant, and thus the term between brackets on the left-hand side of (5) is zero. We may therefore write (5) as:

$$s_1^* = - (q_{s2}\, \varphi_{12} + \ldots + q_{sn}\, \varphi_{1n})\, p_1 + q_{s2}\, \varphi_{12} p_2 + \ldots +$$
$$+ q_{sn}\, \varphi_{1n} p_n \cdot \ldots \ldots \ldots \ldots \ldots \ldots \ldots \ldots \ldots \quad (6)$$

(s_1^* represents the relative change in S_1 as a result of the substitution effect).

Apart from a substitution effect, the price changes also have an effect on income. This income effect indicates by what percentage the demand (in terms of volume) for a particular product will rise or fall if real income rises or falls by 1%. Or, which amounts to the same thing, if the average price level, at a constant nominal income, falls or rises by one per cent. This average change in price can be calculated by weighting the price changes of the individual types of products with the corresponding value shares, i.e. with the share of each relevant commodity in the market. Let μ_i be the elasticity of income for a product i. In the equation which gives the relation between a percentage change in the demand for product i and the average percentage change in price, this elasticity must then be given a minus sign, since the effect on real income of a rise in price is negative and the effect of a fall in price is positive.

The relative change in the demand for product 1 as a result of the income effect (symbolized by s**) is therefore:

$$s_1^{**} = - \mu_1 (q_{s1}\, p_1 + q_{s2}\, p_2 + \ldots \ldots \ldots + q_{sn}\, p_n) \cdot \ldots \ldots \quad (7)$$

The total change as a result of the price changes is:

$$s_1 = s_1^* + s_1^{**} = - (q_{s1}\, \mu_1 + q_{s2}\, \varphi_{12} + \ldots + q_{sn}\, \varphi_{1n})\, p_1 -$$
$$- q_{s2}\, (\mu_1 - \varphi_{12})\, p_2 - \ldots - q_{sn}\, (\mu_1 - \varphi_{1n})\, p_n \cdot \ldots \ldots \quad (8)$$

From (8) we can derive the direct and indirect elasticities of demand
The direct elasticity of demand is:

$$_1\eta_1 = -(q_{s1}\,\mu_1 + q_{s2}\,\varphi_{12} + \cdots + q_{sn}\,\varphi_{1n})$$

and the indirect elasticities of demand are:

$$_2\eta_1 = -q_{s2}\,(\mu_1 - \varphi_{12})$$

- -

$$_n\eta_1 = -q_{sn}\,(\mu_1 - \varphi_{1n})$$

These elasticities satisfy the condition that the sum of the income
elasticity and the direct and indirect elasticities of demand should be zero.
Generally formulated the above equations read:

$$-\varphi_{ij} = \frac{d\dfrac{S_i}{S_j}}{\dfrac{S_i}{S_j}} : \frac{d\dfrac{P_i}{P_j}}{\dfrac{P_i}{P_j}} \quad \cdots \cdots \cdots \cdots \cdots \tag{1}$$

$$(i=1,2..)\,j\,(..n)$$
$$(j=1,2..)\,i\,(..n)$$

$$s_i - s_j = -\varphi_{ij}\,(p_i - p_j) \cdots \cdots \cdots \cdots \cdots \tag{2}$$

$$q_{sj}\,(s_i - s_j) = -q_{sj}\,\varphi_{ij}\,(p_i - p_j) \cdots \cdots \cdots \cdots \tag{3}$$

$$\sum_{\substack{j=1 \\ j \neq i}}^{n} q_{sj}\,(s_i - s_j) = \sum_{\substack{j=1 \\ j \neq i}}^{n} -q_{sj}\,\varphi_{ij}\,(p_i - p_j) \cdots \cdots \cdots \tag{4}$$

$$s_i - q_{si}\,s_i - \sum_{\substack{j=1 \\ j \neq i}}^{n} q_{sj}\,s_j = -\sum_{\substack{j=1 \\ j \neq i}}^{n} q_{sj}\,\varphi_{ij}\,p_i + \sum_{\substack{j=1 \\ j \neq i}}^{n} q_{sj}\,\varphi_{ij}\,p_j \quad \cdots \tag{5}$$

$$s_i^* = -\sum_{\substack{j=1 \\ j \neq i}}^{n} q_{sj}\,\varphi_{ij}\,p_i + \sum_{\substack{j=1 \\ j \neq i}}^{n} q_{sj}\,\varphi_{ij}\,p_j \cdots \cdots \cdots \cdots \tag{6}$$

$$s_i^{**} = -\mu_i \sum_{\substack{j=1 \\ j \neq i}}^{n} q_{sj}\,p_j \cdots \cdots \cdots \cdots \cdots \cdots \cdots \tag{7}$$

$$s_i = s_i^* + s_i^{**} = -\left(q_{si}\,\mu_i + \sum_{\substack{j=1 \\ j \neq i}}^{n} q_{sj}\varphi_{ij}\right) p_i - \sum_{\substack{j=1 \\ j \neq i}}^{n} q_{sj}\,(\mu_i - \varphi_{ij})\,p_j. \tag{8}$$

If we assume that all φ terms are equal to the average φ and all μ terms
are equal to the average μ the direct elasticities of demand are thus:

$$_i\eta_i = -q_{si}\,\mu - (1 - q_{si})\,\varphi$$

and the indirect elasticities of demand

$$_j\eta_i = - q_{sj} (\mu - \varphi)$$

It is plain from these formulae that, if $\varphi = \mu = 1$, the direct elasticity of demand is -1 and the indirect elasticities of demand 0.

Relation between changes in value and changes in volume

If φ_{12} is the elasticity of substitution for product 1 in relation to product 2, then:

$$\frac{S_1}{S_2} = A \left(\frac{P_1}{P_2}\right)^{-\varphi_{12}} \quad \cdots\cdots\cdots\cdots\cdots \quad (1)$$

where A is a constant. Likewise:

$$\frac{S_1 P_1}{S_2 P_2} = A \left(\frac{P_1}{P_2}\right)^{1-\varphi_{12}} \quad \cdots\cdots\cdots\cdots \quad (2)$$

or

$$\log (S_1 P_1) - \log (S_2 P_2) = \log A + (1-\varphi_{12}) (\log P_1 - \log P) . \quad (3)$$

hence

$$\frac{d\{\log (S_1 P_1) - \log (S_2 P_2)\}}{d (\log P_1 - \log P_2)} = (1-\varphi_{12}) \cdots\cdots \quad (4)$$

or

$$\frac{d (S_1 P_1)}{S_1 P_1} - \frac{d (S_2 P_2)}{S_2 P_2} = (1-\varphi_{12}) \left(\frac{d P_1}{P_1} - \frac{d P_2}{P_2}\right) \cdots \quad (5)$$

This can be written as

$$\bar{s}_1 - \bar{s}_2 = (1-\varphi_{12})(p_1 - p_2) \cdots\cdots\cdots\cdots \quad (6)$$

Multiplying both sides by the value share q_{s2} gives

$$q_{s2} \bar{s}_1 - q_{s2} \bar{s}_2 = (1-\varphi_{12}) q_{s2} (p_1 - p_2) \cdots\cdots\cdots \quad (7)$$

likewise

$$q_{s3} \bar{s}_1 - q_{s3} \bar{s}_3 = (1-\varphi_{13}) q_{s3} (p_1 - p_3)$$

$$\frac{q_{sn} \bar{s}_1 - q_{sn} \bar{s}_n = (1-\varphi_{1n}) q_{sn} (p_1 - p_n)}{}$$

$$+$$

$$(1-q_{s1}) \bar{s}_1 - q_{s2} \bar{s}_2 - q_{s3} \bar{s}_3 - \cdots - q_{sn} \bar{s}_n =$$
$$= (1-\varphi_{12}) q_{s2} (p_1 - p_2) + (1-\varphi_{13}) q_{s3} (p_1 - p_3) +$$
$$+ \cdots + (1-\varphi_{1n}) q_{sn} (p_1 - p_n) \cdots\cdots\cdots \quad (8)$$

Since the total expenditure remains unchanged, the weighted sum of the relative changes of value is zero. On the left-hand side of (8), then, only the term $\bar{s}_1$ remains. If we further assume that all φ terms are equal to the average φ, then (8) becomes:

$$\bar{s}_1 = (1 - \varphi)(1 - q_{s1})\,p_1 - (1 - \varphi)\,q_{s2}\,p_2 - $$
$$- (1 - \varphi)\,q_{s3}\,p_3 - \cdots - (1 - \varphi)\,q_{sn}\,p_n \cdot \cdot \cdot \cdot \cdot \cdot \quad (9)$$

The direct elasticity of the value of the expenditure on product 1 is thus:

$$_1\bar{\eta}_1 = (1 - \varphi)(1 - q_{s1}) = 1 - (q_{s1} \cdot 1 + q_{s2}\,\varphi + q_{s3}\,\varphi + \cdots + q_{sn}\,\varphi)$$

and the indirect elasticities are:

$$_2\bar{\eta}_1 = -(1 - \varphi)\,q_{s2}$$
$$_n\bar{\eta}_1 = -(1 - \varphi)\,q_{sn}$$

The 'value elasticities' are denoted here by $\bar{\eta}$. The relation between $\bar{\eta}$ and η is very simple: the direct 'value elasticity' is one greater than the direct 'volume elasticity', whilst the indirect elasticities of value and volume are equal to one another, at least if $\mu = 1$, which we have assumed throughout.

Nevertheless, the relation between change in value and change in volume is unfortunately more complicated than the foregoing paragraph suggests. Briefly, it amounts to the fact that the volume change, directly calculated with the 'volume elasticity', neglects second-order effects which are not neglected if the volume changes are calculated via the changes in value. This can be demonstrated as follows. The change in value is:

$$d(S_1 P_1) = S_1\,dP_1 + P_1\,dS_1 + dS_1\,dP_1 \cdot \cdot \cdot \cdot \cdot \cdot \cdot \quad (1)$$

Dividing by $(S_1 P_1)$ gives, after some simplification:

$$\bar{s}_1 = p_1 + s_1 + p_1 s_1 = p_1 + (1 + p_1)\,s_1 \cdot \cdot \cdot \cdot \cdot \cdot \cdot \cdot \quad (2)$$

or

$$s_1 = \frac{\bar{s}_1 - p_1}{1 + p_1} \quad \cdot \cdot \cdot \cdot \cdot \cdot \cdot \cdot \cdot \cdot \quad (3)$$

If both p_1 and $\bar{s}_1$ are unknown we thus obtain, if we do *not* neglect secondary effects, non-linear equations. The equations become linear again, however, if we ignore the secondary effects. The equation

$$s_1 = \bar{s}_1 - p_1 \quad \cdot \cdot \cdot \cdot \cdot \cdot \cdot \cdot \cdot \cdot \cdot \cdot \quad (4)$$

can now be written as:

$$s_1 = {}_1\bar{\eta}_1 p_1 + {}_2\bar{\eta}_1 p_2 + \cdots + {}_n\bar{\eta}_1 p_n - p_1 \quad\cdots\cdots\quad (5)$$

where

$$ {}_1\bar{\eta}_1 p_1 - p_1 = ({}_1\bar{\eta}_1 - 1)\, p_1 = {}_1\eta_1 p_1 \quad\cdots\cdots\cdots\quad (6) $$

The indirect 'value elasticities' are always equal to the 'volume elasticities'. We may therefore conclude that the volume change, calculated with the 'volume elasticity', disregards the secondary effects because only then is the direct 'volume elasticity' one smaller than the direct 'value elasticity'.

In the three phases of our customs union model the price changes in the first and second phase are given. The models thus remain linear even if the secondary effects are not neglected. Only in the third phase, when calculating the changes in the terms of trade designed to restore equilibrium, are the prices unknown. In the third phase we have therefore ignored second-order effects and have calculated the volume changes with the aid of the 'volume elasticities'.

Imposition and abolition of import duties (in the first and second phases)

Upon the *imposition* of import duties the prices in the initial situation are equal to unity, and the absolute and relative changes in the price of the *import goods* are equal to the tariff t.

The relative change in volume is thus:

$$ s = \frac{\bar{s} - p}{1 + p} = \frac{\bar{s} - t}{1 + t} $$

and the absolute change:

$$ Ss = \frac{\bar{S}\bar{s} - \lfloor St}{1 + t}. $$

Upon the *abolition* of import duties the prices of the *import goods* in the initial situation are $(1 + t)$. The absolute change in price is $-t$ and the relative change in price is $\dfrac{-t}{1 + t}$.

The absolute change in value is:

$$ d\,(SP) = S\,d\,P + P\,d\,S + d\,P\,d\,S = S\,d\,P + (1 + t)\,d\,S - {} $$
$$ -\,t\,d\,S = S\,d\,P + d\,S. $$

10

Since the absolute change is equal to the product of relative change and initial value, we may also write:

$$d\,(S\,P) = \bar{S}\,\bar{s} = S\,d\,P + d\,S = S\,P\!p + S\,s$$

Therefore the absolute change in volume is:

$$S\,s = \bar{S}\,\bar{s} - S\,P\!p.$$

As far as the *export product* is concerned, there is no difficulty at all in either case. Since the price of the export product is unity and does not alter, the change in volume is equal to the change in value.

DERIVATION OF ELASTICITIES OF SUPPLY

The derivation of the direct and indirect elasticities of supply is similar to the derivation of the elasticities of demand. Starting from the definition of the elasticity of substitution of supply:

$$\delta_{12} = \frac{d\dfrac{X_1}{X_2}}{\dfrac{X_1}{X_2}} : \frac{d\dfrac{P_1}{P_2}}{\dfrac{P_1}{P_2}} = \frac{x_1 - x_2}{p_1 - p_2} \quad \cdots \cdots \cdots \cdots \quad (1)$$

we can again give the complete set of definitions for the elasticities of supply relating to the product 1:

$$x_1 - x_2 = \delta_{12}(p_1 - p_2)$$
$$x_1 - x_3 = \delta_{13}(p_1 - p_3)$$
$$\text{-----------------------------------}$$
$$x_1 - x_n = \delta_{1n}(p_1 - p_n) \quad \cdots \cdots \cdots \cdots \quad (2)$$

We multiply both sides with the pertaining production share, i.e. the share represented by the value of the production of a certain product in the total value of the products.

$$q_{x2}(x_1 - x_2) = q_{x2}\,\delta_{12}(p_1 - p_2)$$
$$q_{x3}(x_1 - x_3) = q_{x3}\,\delta_{13}(p_1 - p_3)$$
$$\text{-----------------------------------}$$
$$q_{xn}(x_1 - x_n) = q_{xn}\,\delta_{1n}(p_1 - p_n) \quad \cdots \cdots \cdots \cdots \quad (3)$$

Summation gives:

$$(q_{x2} + q_{x3} + \cdots + q_{xn})\,x_1 - q_{x2}\,x_2 - \cdots - q_{xn}\,x_n =$$
$$(q_{x2}\,\delta_{12} + \cdots + q_{xn}\,\delta_{1n})\,p_1 - q_{x2}\,\delta_{12}\,p_2 - \cdots - q_{xn}\,\delta_{1n}\,p_n \quad (4)$$

$$x_1 - (q_{x1}\,x_1 + q_{x2}\,x_2 + \cdots + q_{xn}\,x_n) = (q_{x2}\,\delta_{12} + \cdots \cdots +$$
$$+ q_{xn}\,\delta_{1n})\,p_1 - q_{x2}\,\delta_{12}\,p_2 - \cdots - q_{xn}\,\delta_{1n}\,p_n \quad \cdots \cdots \quad (5)$$

Since the total supply remains unchanged, and hence the weighted sum of the relative changes is zero, the term between brackets on the left side is equal to zero.

10*

* See p. 51

$$x_1 = (q_{x2}\,\delta_{12} + q_{x3}\,\delta_{13} + \cdots + q_{xn}\,\delta_{1n})\,p_1 - q_{x2}\,\delta_{12}\,p_2 -$$
$$- q_{x3}\,\delta_{13}\,p_3 - \cdots - q_{xn}\,\delta_{1n}\,p_n \cdots \cdots \cdots \cdots \quad (6)$$

Since, in the case of supply, the income effect is irrelevant, we can immediately find from (6) the direct and indirect elasticities of supply. Direct elasticities of supply:

$$_1\alpha_1 = q_{x2}\,\delta_{12} + q_{x3}\,\delta_{13} + \cdots + q_{xn}\,\delta_{1n}$$

Indirect elasticities of supply:

$$_2\alpha_1 = -\,q_{x2}\,\delta_{12}$$

$$_3\alpha_1 = -\,q_{x3}\,\delta_{13}$$

$$\text{-----------------------------}$$

$$_n\alpha_1 = -\,q_{xn}\,\delta_{1n}$$

Generally formulated the above equations read:

$$\delta_{ij} = \frac{d\dfrac{X_i}{X_j}}{\dfrac{X_i}{X_j}} : \frac{d\dfrac{P_i}{P_j}}{\dfrac{P_i}{P_j}} = \frac{x_i - x_j}{p_i - p_j} \cdots \qquad \left.\begin{array}{c}\\ \\ \\ \\ \\ \\ \\ \\ \\ \\ \\ \end{array}\right\} \cdots \cdots \cdots \cdots \quad (1)$$

$$\begin{array}{l}(i = 1,2\,..)\,j\,(..n)\\(j = 1,2\,..)\,i\,(..n)\end{array}$$

$$x_i - x_j = \delta_{ij}\,(p_i - p_j) \cdots \cdots \cdots \cdots \quad (2)$$

$$q_{xj}\,(x_i - x_j) = q_{xj}\,\delta_{ij}\,(p_i - p_j) \cdots \quad (3)$$

$$\sum_{\substack{j=1\\j\neq i}}^{n} q_{xj}\,(x_i - x_j) = \sum_{\substack{j=1\\j\neq i}}^{n} q_{xj}\,\delta_{ij}\,(p_i - p_j) \cdots \cdots \cdots \quad (4)$$

$$x_i - q_{xi}\,x_i - \sum_{\substack{j=1\\j\neq i}}^{n} q_{xj}\,x_j = \sum_{\substack{j=1\\j\neq i}}^{n} q_{xj}\,\delta_{ij}\,p_i - \sum_{\substack{j=1\\j\neq i}}^{n} q_{xj}\,\delta_{ij}\,p_j \cdots \quad (5)$$

$$x_i = \sum_{\substack{j=1\\j\neq i}}^{n} q_{xj}\,\delta_{ij}\,p_i - \sum_{\substack{j=1\\j\neq i}}^{n} q_{xj}\,\delta_{ij}\,p_j \cdots \cdots \cdots \cdots \quad (6)$$

The direct elasticities of supply are thus:

$$_i\alpha_i = \sum_{\substack{j=1\\j\neq i}}^{n} q_{xj}\,\delta_{ij}$$

The indirect elasticities of supply are:

$$_j\alpha_i = -\,q_{xj}\,\delta_{ij}$$

If we assume that all δ_{ij} terms are equal to the average elasticity of substitution, then $_i\alpha_i = (1 - q_{xi})\, \delta$.

'Volume elasticity' and 'value elasticity' in respect of supply

In the same way as in the case of the elasticities of demand, we can also calculate the 'value elasticities' for the supply.

If δ_{12} is the elasticity of substitution in respect of the supply of product 1 in relation to product 2, then:

$$\frac{X_1}{X_2} = A \left(\frac{P_1}{P_2}\right)^{\delta_{12}} \qquad \qquad (1)$$

$$\frac{X_1 P_1}{X_2 P_2} = A \left(\frac{P_1}{P_2}\right)^{\delta_{12}+1} \qquad \qquad (2)$$

$$\log (X_1 P_1) - \log (X_2 P_2) = \log A + (\delta_{12}+1)(\log P_1 - \log P_2) \quad (3)$$

$$\frac{d\{\log (X_1 P_1) - \log (X_2 P_2)\}}{d (\log P_1 - \log P_2)} = \delta_{12} + 1 \qquad (4)$$

$$\bar{x}_1 - \bar{x}_2 = (\delta_{12} + 1)(p_1 - p_2) \qquad \qquad (5)$$

$$q_{x2}(\bar{x}_1 - \bar{x}_2) = (\delta_{12} + 1)\, q_{x2}(p_1 - p_2)$$
$$q_{x3}(\bar{x}_1 - \bar{x}_0) = (\delta_{13} + 1)\, q_{x3}(p_1 \quad p_3)$$

$$\frac{q_{xn}(\bar{x}_1 - \bar{x}_n) = (\delta_{1n} + 1)\, q_{xn}(p_1 - p_n)}{} \qquad (6)$$

$$(1 - q_{x1})\, \bar{x}_1 - q_{x2}\, \bar{x}_2 - \ldots - q_{xn}\, \bar{x}_n =$$
$$= (\delta_{12} + 1)\, q_{x2}(p_1 - p_2) + \ldots + q_{xn}(p_1 - p_n) \quad \ldots \quad (7)$$

or, if we make the δ_{ij} terms all equal to the average δ,

$$\bar{x}_1 - q_{x1}\,\bar{x}_1 - q_{x2}\,\bar{x}_2 - \ldots - q_{xn}\,\bar{x}_n = (\delta + 1)(1 - q_{x1})\, p_1 -$$
$$- (\delta + 1)\, q_{x2}\, p_2 - \ldots - (\delta + 1)\, q_{xn}\, p_n = [\delta (1 - q_{x1}) + 1]\, p_1 -$$
$$- \delta q_{x2}\, p_2 - \ldots - \delta q_{xn}\, p_n - q_{x1}\, p_1 - q_{x2}\, p_2 - \ldots - q_{xn}\, p_n \quad (8)$$

Since the average change in volume is zero, the average change in value is equal to the average change in price. Equation (8) thus becomes:

$$\bar{x}_1 = [\delta (1 - q_{x1}) + 1]\, p_1 - \delta q_{x2}\, p_2 - \ldots - \delta q_{xn}\, p_n. \quad (9)$$

10**

The direct elasticity of value is therefore:

$$_1\bar{\alpha}_1 = \delta\,(1 - q_{x1}) + 1$$

and the indirect elasticities:

$$_2\bar{\alpha}_1 = -\,\delta q_{x2}$$

$$\overline{\phantom{_2\bar{\alpha}_1 = -\,\delta q_{x2}}}$$

$$_n\bar{\alpha}_1 = -\,\delta q_{xn}$$

The direct 'value elasticity' in respect of supply is thus here, too, one greater than the 'volume elasticity'.

DERIVATION OF THE ELASTICITY OF IMPORTS

TWO-COUNTRY MODEL

The elasticity of imports indicates the percentage increase in imports when the ratio of the import price level to the level of the national (export) product changes by one per cent. It is not a fundamental datum, but is determined by the fundamental elasticities, namely the elasticities of substitution of supply and demand and the elasticities of income, and further by the structure of production and expenditure.

In calculating the various relationships we shall make use of the ordinary symbols. The C product is the export commodity of country 1 and the competitive home-market commodity of country 2, whilst the I product is the export commodity of country 2 and the competitive home-market commodity of country 1. We shall also use the following value-share concepts:

$$q_{yc} = \frac{X_c P_c}{S_c P_c + S_i P_i} \qquad q_{yi} = \frac{X_i P_i}{S_c P_c + S_i P_i}$$

$$q_{xc} = \frac{X_c P_c}{X_c P_c + X_i P_i} \qquad q_{xi} = \frac{X_i P_i}{X_c P_c + X_i P_i}$$

$$q_m = \frac{M_i P_i}{S_c P_c + S_i P_i} \qquad q_f = \frac{F_c P_c}{S_c P_c + S_i P_i}$$

$$q_{sc} = \frac{S_c P_c}{S_c P_c + S_i P_i} \qquad q_{si} = \frac{S_i P_i}{S_c P_c + S_i P_i}$$

The distinction between q_y and q_x is relevant only if an import duty is already imposed in the initial situation, or if the balance of payments is not in equilibrium.

We confine ourselves here to a two-country model and consider the elasticity of imports for country 1. The superscripts may therefore be omitted. Since the imports represent the difference between home consumption and home production of the I commodity, the change in real expenditure (as a result of price changes) will be derived first, after which we shall find the change in production.

$$s_i = q_{sc} \, \varphi \, (p_c - p_i) - \mu_i \, (q_{sc} \, p_c + q_{si} \, p_i) +$$
$$+ \, \mu_i \, (q_{yc} \, p_c + q_{yi} \, p_i + q_m \, t_i) \, \ldots \ldots \ldots \ldots \ldots \ldots \quad (1)$$

The first term on the right-hand side is derived from the definition of the elasticity of substitution:

$$(s_c - s_i) \equiv - \, \varphi \, (p_c - p_i) \, \ldots \ldots \ldots \ldots \ldots \ldots \quad (1a)$$

combined with the equilibrium condition:

$$- \frac{d \, S_i}{d \, S_c} = \frac{P_c}{P_i} \quad \ldots \ldots \ldots \ldots \ldots \ldots \ldots \ldots \quad (2a)$$

This condition expresses that, in a situation of equilibrium, the price ratio is equal to the marginal ratio of substitution of demand. Multiplying both sides by $\frac{S_i}{S_c}$, then (2a) gives:

$$- \frac{d \, S_i}{S_i} \cdot \frac{P_i \, S_i}{P_c \, S_c} = \frac{d \, S_c}{S_c} \quad \ldots \ldots \ldots \ldots \ldots \ldots \quad (2b)$$

$$- \, s_i \frac{P_i \, S_i}{P_c \, S_c} = s_c \, \ldots \ldots \ldots \ldots \ldots \ldots \ldots \ldots \quad (2c)$$

It then follows from (1a) and (2c) that

$$- \, s_i \frac{P_i \, S_i}{P_c \, S_c} - s_i = - \, \varphi \, (p_c - p_i) \, \ldots \ldots \ldots \ldots \quad (3a)$$

$$s_i = \frac{P_c \, S_c}{P_c \, S_c + P_i \, S_i} \cdot \varphi \, (p_c - p_i) = q_{sc} \, \varphi \, (p_c - p_i) \, \ldots \quad (3b)$$

The second term on the right-hand side of equation (1) gives the effect of the price change on real income where nominal income remains the same, whilst the third term gives the effect of the changing nominal income. By algebraic manipulation, in which we successively substitute the relations existing between the value shares ($q_m = q_f$ and $q_{sc} = 1 - q_{yi} - q_m$) equation (1) is transformed into (1'):

$$s_i = q_{sc} \, \varphi \, (p_c - p_i) - \mu_i \, \{(q_{sc} - q_{yc}) \, p_c + (q_{si} - q_{yi}) \, p_i - q_m \, t_i\}$$
$$s_i = q_{sc} \, \varphi \, (p_c - p_i) - \mu_i \, (- q_m \, p_c + q_m \, p_i) + \mu_i \, q_m \, t_i$$
$$s_i = q_{sc} \, \varphi \, (p_c - p_i) + \mu_i \, q_m \, (p_c - p_i) + \mu_i \, q_m \, t_i$$
$$s_i = \{(1 - q_{yi} - q_m) \, \varphi + \mu_i \, q_m\} \, (p_c - p_i) + \mu_i \, q_m \, t_i \, \ldots \quad (1')$$

Next, we consider the relative change in production as a result of the price changes.

$$x_i = - q_{xc} \, \delta \, (p_c - p_i) = - (1 - q_{xi}) \, \delta \, (p_c - p_i) \; \cdot \; \cdot \; \cdot \; \cdot \quad (2)$$

This equation is derived from the definition of the elasticity of substitution of supply, combined with the equilibrium condition.

$$- \frac{d \, X_i}{d \, X_c} = \frac{P_c}{P_i}.$$

The definition of the relative change in imports is:

$$m_i = \frac{S_i \, s_i - X_i \, x_i}{S_i - X_i} = \frac{S_i}{M_i} \, s_i - \frac{X_i}{M_i} \, x_i \; \cdot \; \cdot \; \cdot \; \cdot \; \cdot \; \cdot \; \cdot \; \cdot \quad (3)$$

Dividing numerator and denominator of the fractions in (3) by the income, we find:

$$m_i = \frac{q_{si}}{q_m} \, s_i - \frac{q_{yi}}{q_m} \, x_i = \frac{q_{yi} + q_m}{q_m} \, s_i - \frac{q_{yi}}{q_m} \, x_i \; \cdot \; \cdot \; \cdot \; \cdot \; \cdot \quad (3')$$

Substitution of (1') and (2) in (3') gives:

$$m_i = \frac{q_{yi} + q_m}{q_m} \, [\{(1 - q_{yi} - q_m) \, \varphi + \mu_i \, q_m\} \, (p_c - p_i)] +$$

$$+ \, (q_{yi} + q_m) \, \mu_i \, t_i + \frac{q_{yi}}{q_m} \, (1 - q_{xi}) \, \delta \, (p_c - p_i) \; \cdot \; \cdot \; \cdot \; \cdot \; \cdot \quad (4)$$

We may also write (4) as:

$$m_i = \varepsilon_m \, (p_c - p_i) + (q_{yi} + q_m) \, \mu_i \, t_i \; \cdot \; \cdot \; \cdot \; \cdot \; \cdot \; \cdot \; \cdot \; \cdot \quad (5)$$

or

$$m_i = - \, \varepsilon_m \, (p_i - p_c) + (q_{yi} + q_m) \, \mu_i \, t_i$$

This equation states that the relative change in imports is in the first place a function of the relative change in the price ratio, and in the second place that it depends on a change in nominal income as a result of a tariff change. The factor $- \varepsilon_m$ indicates by what percentage the imports change if the relative price change $(p_i - p_c)$ is 1 %, which is no other than the definition of the elasticity of imports.

From (4) and (5) we thus find:

$$\varepsilon_m = \frac{q_{yi} + q_m}{q_m} \left[(1 - q_{yi} - q_m)\, \varphi + \mu_i\, q_m \right] + \frac{q_{yi}}{q_m} (1 - q_{xi})\, \delta \quad . \quad . \quad (6)$$

The result found here leads to an important conclusion.

If we insert in the formula arrived at for the smallest possible average elasticities of substitution, namely $\delta = 0$ and $\varphi = 1$, we can then show that the average elasticity of imports is always greater than or at least equal to unity. This does not alter the fact that the elasticity of imports for certain commodities may still be smaller than unity, but it is certainly not acceptable to assume with Verdoorn that the average elasticity of imports is 0.5.

In a similar way we can also find the elasticity of exports. The interested and indulgent reader may try the calculation himself; we shall give here merely the key equations:

$$s_c = q_{si}\, \varphi\, (p_i - p_c) - \mu_c\, (q_{sc}\, p_c + q_{si}\, p_i) +$$
$$+ \mu_c\, (q_{yc}\, p_c + q_{yi}\, p_i + q_m\, t_i) \cdot \ldots \ldots \ldots \ldots \quad (1)$$

$$s_c = \left\{ (q_{yi} + q_m)\, \varphi - \mu_c\, q_m \right\} (p_i - p_c) + \mu_c\, q_m\, t_i \ldots \ldots \quad (1')$$

$$x_c = - q_{xi}\, \delta\, (p_i - p_c) \cdot \ldots \ldots \ldots \ldots \ldots \quad (2)$$

$$f_c = \frac{X_c\, x_c - S_c\, s_c}{F_c} = \frac{1 - q_{yi}}{q_m}\, x_c - \frac{1 - q_{xi} - q_m}{q_m}\, s_c \ldots \quad (3)$$

$$f_c = - \frac{1 - q_{yi}}{q_m}\, q_{xi}\, \delta\, (p_i - p_c) - \frac{1 - q_{yi} - q_m}{q_m} \cdot$$
$$\cdot \left\{ (q_{yi} + q_m)\, \varphi - \mu_c\, q_m \right\} (p_i - p_c) - (1 - q_{yi} - q_m)\, \mu_c\, t_i \ldots \quad (4)$$

$$\varepsilon_f = \frac{1 - q_{yi} - q_m}{q_m} \left\{ (q_{yi} + q_m)\, \varphi - \mu_c\, q_m \right\} + \frac{1 - q_{yi}}{q_m}\, q_{xi}\, \delta \quad . \quad . \quad (5)$$

MODELS FOR THE CUSTOMS UNION OF THE E.E.C.

COMPLETE SPECIALIZATION

First Phase

$$\Delta^* \bar{S}_j^i = S_j^i P_j^i \left\{ \left(\sum_{k=1}^{6} {}_k \bar{\eta}_j^i p_k^i \right) - \mu \, q_m^i \, t^i \right\} \quad \ldots \ldots \quad (1)$$

$$\Delta^* S_j^i = \Delta \bar{S}_j^i - S_j^i P_j^i p_j^i \qquad \begin{matrix} (i = 1.2 \ldots 5) \\ (j = 1.2 \ldots 6) \end{matrix} \quad \ldots \ldots \quad (2)$$

$$p_i^i = 0 \quad \ldots \ldots \ldots \ldots \ldots \ldots \ldots \ldots \ldots \quad (3)$$

$$p_j^i = \frac{t^i}{1 + t^i} \qquad (i \neq j) \quad \ldots \ldots \ldots \ldots \ldots \quad (4)$$

Second Phase

$$\Delta^{**} S_j^i = S_j^i \left({}_6 \eta_j^i p_6^i + \mu \, q_{m6}^i \, t_6^i \right) \qquad \begin{matrix} (i = 1,2 \ldots 5) \\ (j = 1,2 \ldots 6) \end{matrix} \quad \ldots \ldots \quad (5)$$

$$p_6^i = t_6^i \quad \ldots \ldots \ldots \ldots \ldots \ldots \ldots \ldots \quad (6)$$

Third Phase

$$\sum_{i=1}^{6} \left(\Delta^* S_j^i + \Delta^{**} S_j^i + S_j^i s_j^i \right) = 0 \quad (j = 1,2 \ldots 5) \quad \ldots \ldots \quad (7)$$

$$s_j^i = \sum_{k=1}^{5} \left({}_k \eta_j^i p_j + \mu \, p_i \right) \qquad \begin{matrix} (i = 1,2 \ldots 5) \\ (j = 1,2 \ldots 5) \end{matrix} \quad \ldots \ldots \quad (8)$$

$$s_j^6 = m_j^6 = \beta \, p_j \qquad (j = 1,2 \ldots 5) \quad \ldots \ldots \quad (9)$$

The symbols provided with a single asterisk denote the changes resulting from the abolition of all import duties (first phase) and the symbols provided with two asterisks denote the changes resulting from the imposition of the external tariff (second phase).

INCOMPLETE SPECIALIZATION

First Phase

$$\Delta^* \bar{X}^i_j = X^i_j P^i_j \sum_{k=1}^{5} {}_k\bar{\alpha}^i_j p^i_j \ldots \ldots \ldots \ldots \ldots \quad (1)$$

$$\Delta^* X^i_j = \Delta^* \bar{X}^i_j - X^i_j P^i_j p^i_j \ldots \ldots \ldots \ldots \quad (2)$$

$$\Delta^* \bar{S}^i_j = S^i_j P^i_j \left\{ \left(\sum_{k=1}^{5} {}_k\bar{\eta}^i_j p^i_j \right) + \mu y^i \right\} {(i = 1,2 \ldots 5) \atop (j = 1,2 \ldots 6)} \cdots \quad (3)$$

$$\Delta^* S^i_j = \Delta^* \bar{S}^i_j - S^i_j P^i_j p^i_j \ldots \ldots \ldots \ldots \ldots \quad (4)$$

$$y^i = \left(\sum_{j=1}^{5} q^i_{yj} p^i_j \right) + q^i_m t^i \qquad (i = 1,2 \ldots 5) \cdots \quad (5)$$

$$p^i_i = 0 \quad (i = 1.2 \ldots 5) \ldots \ldots \ldots \ldots \ldots \quad (6)$$

$$p^i_j = \frac{-t^i}{1 + t^i} \qquad\qquad {(i = 1,2 \ldots 5) \atop (j = 1,2 \ldots 6)} \cdots \quad (7)$$

Second Phase

$$\Delta^{**} X^i_j = X^i_j {}_6\alpha^i_j p^i_6 \ldots \ldots \ldots \ldots \ldots \ldots \quad (8)$$

$$\Delta^{**} S^i_j = S^i_j ({}_6\eta^i_j p^i_6 + \mu y^i) \ldots \ldots \ldots \ldots \quad (9)$$

$$\qquad\qquad\qquad\qquad\qquad {(i = 1,2 \ldots 5) \atop (j = 1,2 \ldots 6)}$$

$$y^i = q^i_{y6} p^i_6 + q^i_{m6} t^i_6 \ldots \ldots \ldots \ldots \ldots \ldots \quad (10)$$

$$p^i_6 = t^i_6 \ldots \ldots \ldots \ldots \ldots \ldots \ldots \ldots \ldots \quad (11)$$

Third Phase

$$\sum_{i=1}^{6} (\Delta^* X^i_j + \Delta^{**} X^i_j - \Delta^* S^i_j - \Delta^{**} S^i_j + X^i_j x^i_j -$$

$$- S^i_j s^i_j) = 0 \qquad\qquad (j = 1,2 \ldots 5) \cdots \quad (12)$$

$$x^i_j = \sum_{k=1}^{5} {}_k\alpha^i_j p_k \qquad {(i = 1,2 \ldots 5) \atop (j = 1,2 \ldots 5)} \cdots \quad (13)$$

$$s^i_j = (\sum_{k=1}^{5} {}_k\eta^i_j p_k) + \mu y^i \ldots \ldots \ldots \ldots \ldots \quad (14)$$

$$y^i = \sum_{j=1}^{5} q^i_{yj} p_j \qquad\qquad (i = 1,2 \ldots 5) \; \ldots \; (15)$$

$$X^6_j x^6_j - S^6_j s^6_j = M^6_j m^6_j = M^6_j \beta p_j \quad (j = 1,2 \ldots 5) \; \ldots \; (16)$$

The remaining variables can be calculated from the following independent equations:

$$x^i_6 = \sum_{k=1}^{5} {}_k\alpha^i_6 p_k \; \ldots\ldots\ldots\ldots\ldots\ldots\ldots \; (17)$$

$$(i = 1,2 \ldots 5)$$

$$s^i_6 = \left(\sum_{k=1}^{5} {}_k\eta^i_6 p_k \right) + \mu \, y^i \; \ldots\ldots\ldots\ldots\ldots \; (18)$$

List of principal symbols

Prices

P_j^i $\quad = \quad$ price of commodity j in country i.

$p_j^i = \dfrac{\Delta P_j^i}{P_j^i}$ $\quad = \quad$ relative change in P_j^i.

P_L^i $\quad = \quad$ wage rate of labour in country i.

Volumes
and Values *

F_j^i $\quad = \quad$ volume of exports of commodity j from country i.

M_j^i $\quad = \quad$ volume of imports of commodity j into country i.

S_j^i $\quad = \quad$ volume of expenditure on commodity j in country i.

$\bar{S}_j^i = S_j^i P_j^i$ $\quad = \quad$ value of expenditure on commodity j in country i.

X_j^i $\quad = \quad$ volume of the production of commodity j in country i.

$\bar{X}_j^i = X_j^i P_j^i$ $\quad = \quad$ value of the production of commodity j in country i.

$\varUpsilon^i$ $\quad = \quad$ value of the national expenditure in country i.

* Capital letters denote absolute quantities, small letters the relative changes in these quantities.

Elasticities (see also pp 66-67)

${}_k\alpha_j^i$	$=$	elasticity of supply of commodity j with reference to the change in the price of commodity k in country i.
β	$=$	share elasticity, or elasticity of outsiders' imports.
δ	$=$	elasticity of substitution of supply.
ε_m^i	$=$	elasticity of imports for country i.
ε_f^i	$=$	elasticity of exports for country i.
${}_k\eta_j^i$	$=$	elasticity of demand for product j with reference to the change in the price of commodity k in country i.
μ	$=$	elasticity of income.
φ	$=$	elasticity of substitution of demand. The symbols provided with the sign − relate to the 'value elasticity'.

Shares

α_j^i	$=$	labour input per unit of product j in country i.
γ^i	$=$	value share of expenditure on the C commodity in country i.
q_m^i	$=$	value of the total imports in country i as a fraction of the total value of expenditure in country i.
q_{mj}^i	$=$	value of the imports of commodity j in country i as a fraction of the total value of expenditure in country i.
q_{sj}^i	$=$	value of expenditure on commodity j in country i as a fraction of the total expenditure in country i.
q_{vj}^i	$=$	value of the imports from country j as a fraction of the total imports of country i.
q_{xj}^i	$=$	value of the production of commodity j as a fraction of the value of the total production in country i.
$q_{yj}^i = \dfrac{X_j P_j^*}{SP}$	$=$	value of the production of commodity j as a fraction of the value of the total expenditure in country i.

* See page 50.